# MASTERING
# WORKPLACE SKILLS:
# WRITING FUNDAMENTALS

# Related Titles

*Mastering Workplace Skills: Grammar Fundamentals*

*Mastering Workplace Skills: Math Fundamentals*

# MASTERING WORKPLACE SKILLS: WRITING FUNDAMENTALS

NEW YORK

Cataloging-in-Publication Data is on file with the Library of Congress.

Printed in the United States of America

9 8 7 6 5 4 3 2 1

First Edition

ISBN 978-1-61103-018-1

For information on LearningExpress, other LearningExpress products, or bulk
sales, please write to us at:
  80 Broad Street
  4th Floor
  New York, NY 10004

Or visit us at:
  www.learningexpressllc.com

# CONTENTS ▶

# CONTENTS

# Introduction

What kind of employee do you want to be? One who struggles to communicate, whose work is sloppy or haphazard and has to be heavily edited—even totally revised—by a colleague? Or do you want to be a dependable, polished professional who is often asked by others for help with projects, from corporate policies to proofreading—the one who can turn out anything from a casual memo to a quarterly report with finesse and an eye for detail? Odds are you'd rather be employee #2, right?

Believe it or not, success in the workplace can sometimes be almost entirely defined by your writing skills. From the moment your resume arrives in an inbox to your last day on the job, the way you present yourself in print carries a lot of weight with employers, colleagues, and clients alike. A sloppy or too-casual email may lead to your first impression being a last one—and a lousy one, at that. A rambling presentation with dense, text-packed slides could be your ticket out of the fast lane. A project proposal that doesn't get to the point until the very last paragraph will probably not make it out of the "read later" pile.

However, you may be reassured to know, great writers are made, not born.

With *Mastering Workplace Skills: Writing Fundamentals*, you've come to the right place. Whether you're bouncing back from a layoff, transitioning from a retail environment to the corporate world, seeking to move up the ladder, returning to the workforce, changing careers, or applying for your very first post-college job, this book will provide you with the skills and strategies to make the most of the opportunities that await you. We have you covered, beginning with the early stages of your job hunt, all the way to your daily workplace writing needs.

This book will help make you into a confident, effective writer, no matter your area of expertise. Get started by reviewing the basics in the **Pretest**. Your results may inspire you to go straight to **Section 4: Grammar Skills** for a primer in grammar and syntax. Let this book be more like a *Choose Your Own Adventure* experience than a read-straight-through slog. Your interests and the areas where you want to improve can drive your progress—don't worry about starting at the beginning and reading all the way to the end.

If you're confident you know a noun from an adjective and can pick a subject-verb disagreement out of a lineup, jump straight to **Section 1: Writing to Get the Job You Want** to get your job search off on the right foot.

From there, it's straight on to building the essential writing skills you need to excel at work. **Section 2** covers **Writing Basics**. Start here if you have always found it difficult to translate your fluid verbal skills into polished prose—you'll make progress once you remember to put your reader first. **Section 3** will introduce you to the **Workplace Writing** you need to know—this may be particularly valuable to career changers or novices to the corporate world. Letters and emails can be particularly tricky, since we write so casually in social correspondence but still adhere to an older code of professionalism in our workplace snail mail. Do presentations make you sweat and see spots? We have some public speaking tips and some PowerPoint advice to put you at ease.

As we mentioned, **Section 4** will take you back to the basics of English grammar, to make sure your writing skills are built upon a solid foundation. **Section 5: The Writing Process** will help you develop the writerly practices of planning, organizing, and revising—but more than that, it will help you harness your unique thinking and learning styles to produce writing that makes the most of your abilities.

It may seem daunting, but even if writing has not been one of your strengths in the past, try not to feel anxious. Every writer you admire began where you are now. Good writers come from good readers who put a lot of time into the editing process. Maybe you feel like you already know how to write, but you still struggle to make a bigger impression at work. There's a good chance you're not bringing all your skills to the forefront. A meeting agenda may not seem like the place to practice polished writing, but if you make the most of every textual communication that comes your way, you'll be on your way to becoming the one everyone wants to ask to look something over. That builds good word of mouth, which may come in handy when you want to apply for a promotion or a special project.

Even if you already have a job, you may want to check on the two bonus **Appendix** sections. **Interviewing for Success** offers advice on how to approach a job interview with confidence and poise. Finally, refer to **Workplace Dos and Don'ts** to see if there's anything you can do to put an even better foot forward.

We want to help you develop your writing skills until you are as dynamic on the page as you are in person. If that sounds good to you, let's get started.

# PRETEST ▶

If you're confident in your reading and writing skills, you can skip this test and go straight to Section 1 to begin polishing your workplace skills right away. However, if you're unsure, if it's been a while since you've studied reading or writing formally, or if you simply want to see how well you score, this diagnostic test contains 50 questions that will measure your baseline knowledge of reading and writing.

Your score will serve as a guide to which areas you need to focus on through the chapters in this book. The answer explanations at the end of the pretest give you a preview of what you'll be learning more thoroughly later on.

Of course, 50 questions can't cover every single concept or rule you will learn by working through these pages, so even if you answer all of the questions on the diagnostic test correctly, there's a good chance you'll find a few ideas or rules in this book that you didn't already know. Correct grammar and punctuation are only the foundation upon which excellent workplace writing skills are built!

# Pretest

**1.** Which version of the sentence is correctly capitalized?

    **a.** Tuesday's panel will include a discussion with deputy Smith, Judge Fuentes, and the Commissioner's assistant, Ray.

    **b.** Tuesday's panel will include a discussion with Deputy Smith, Judge Fuentes, and the commissioner's assistant, Ray.

    **c.** Tuesday's panel will include a discussion with Deputy Smith, judge Fuentes, and the commissioner's assistant, Ray.

    **d.** Tuesday's panel will include a discussion with Deputy Smith, Judge Fuentes, and the Commissioner's Assistant, Ray.

**2.** Which of the underlined words in the following sentence should be capitalized?

The <u>governor</u> gave a speech at the <u>fourth</u> of July picnic, which was held at his <u>cousin's</u> farm five miles <u>east</u> of town.

    **a.** governor

    **b.** fourth

    **c.** cousin's

    **d.** east

**3.** Which of the underlined words in the following sentence should be capitalized?

Last <u>spring</u>, the <u>network broadcast</u> a history special on the Korean <u>war</u>.

**a.** spring
**b.** network
**c.** history
**d.** war

**4.** Which version uses periods correctly?
  **a.** Dr Harrison will speak at a hotel in Chicago, IL, on Thurs at 3:00 P.M.
  **b.** Dr. Harrison will speak at a hotel in Chicago, IL., on Thurs at 3:00 PM.
  **c.** Dr Harrison will speak at a hotel in Chicago, IL., on Thurs. at 3:00 P.M.
  **d.** Dr. Harrison will speak at a hotel in Chicago, IL, on Thurs. at 3:00 P.M.

**5.** Which version uses punctuation correctly?
  **a.** Wow, that was a successful novel? What other books has this author written!
  **b.** Wow! That was a successful novel. What other books has this author written?
  **c.** Wow? That was a successful novel! What other books has this author written?
  **d.** Wow. That was a successful novel? What other books has this author written?

**6.** Which of the following is a sentence fragment, or NOT a complete sentence?

    **a.** Hearing the thunder, the lifeguard ordered the swimmers out of the water.

    **b.** Turn off the printer.

    **c.** Sunday afternoon spent preparing for Monday's big meeting.

    **d.** I was surprised to see that our C.E.O. had written a letter to the editor.

**7.** Three of the following sentences are either run-ons or comma splices. Which one is NOT a faulty sentence?

    **a.** The newspapers are supposed to be delivered by 7:00, but today they didn't arrive until 8:00.

    **b.** I called the caterers this morning, they told me lunch would arrive on time.

    **c.** Look in the supply closet you should find it there.

    **d.** I was the first to sign the petition Harry was second.

**8.** Which version is punctuated correctly?

    **a.** Charlotte, who ran in the Boston Marathon last year will compete in this year's New York Marathon.

    **b.** Charlotte who ran in the Boston Marathon, last year, will compete in this year's New York Marathon.

    **c.** Charlotte who ran in the Boston Marathon last year, will compete in this year's New York Marathon.

    **d.** Charlotte, who ran in the Boston Marathon last year, will compete in this year's New York Marathon.

**9.** Which version is punctuated correctly?
   **a.** The park service will not allow anyone, who does not have a camping permit, to use the campground.
   **b.** The park service will not allow anyone who does not have a camping permit to use the campground.
   **c.** The park service will not allow anyone, who does not have a camping permit to use the campground.
   **d.** The park service will not allow anyone who does not have a camping permit, to use the campground.

**10.** Which version is punctuated correctly?
   **a.** As soon as she finished her dinner, Lisa, who is a volunteer at the hospital, reported for her shift.
   **b.** As soon as she finished her dinner Lisa, who is a volunteer at the hospital reported for her shift.
   **c.** As soon as she finished, her dinner, Lisa who is a volunteer at the hospital, reported for her shift.
   **d.** As soon as she finished her dinner, Lisa who is a volunteer at the hospital reported for her shift.

**11.** Which underlined portion of the following sentence is punctuated incorrectly?

Ms. Sym was born on (**a**) December 15, 1944, in Kingwood, West (**b**) Virginia, when she was (**c**) five, her family moved to (**d**) 347 Benton Street, Zanesville, OH.

   **a.** December 15, 1944,
   **b.** Virginia, when
   **c.** five, her
   **d.** 347 Benton Street, Zanesville, OH

**12.** Which version is punctuated correctly?
   **a.** Yes I would like to review the loan application and please send it as soon as you can to my office.
   **b.** Yes, I would like to review the loan application and please send it, as soon as you can to my office.
   **c.** Yes, I would like to review the loan application and, please send it as soon as you can to my office.
   **d.** Yes, I would like to review the loan application, and please send it as soon as you can to my office.

**13.** Which version is punctuated correctly?
   **a.** It seems, Mr. May, that your shipment has been delayed. We apologize for any inconvenience.
   **b.** It seems Mr. May that your shipment has been delayed we apologize for any inconvenience.
   **c.** It seems, Mr. May, that your shipment has been delayed, we apologize for any inconvenience.
   **d.** It seems Mr. May that your shipment has been delayed. We apologize for any inconvenience.

**14.** Which is the correct punctuation for the underlined portion?

The weather forecasters are predicting 10 inches of snow <u>tonight therefore</u> the annual shareholder's meeting will be rescheduled for next week.

   **a.** tonight, therefore
   **b.** tonight, therefore,
   **c.** tonight; therefore,
   **d.** tonight, therefore;

**15.** Which is the correct punctuation for the underlined portion?

The company will match donations to any two of the following <u>organizations *the*</u> *American Red Cross, Amnesty International,* or the *Cancer Research Institute.*

    **a.** organizations, *the*
    **b.** organizations: *the*
    **c.** organizations; *the*
    **d.** organizations. *the*

**16.** Which version is punctuated correctly?
    **a.** One of my complaints—if you really want to know is that the recycling bins are not clearly labeled.
    **b.** One of my complaints—if you really want to know—is that the recycling bins are not clearly labeled.
    **c.** One of my complaints, if you really want to know—is that the recycling bins are not clearly labeled.
    **d.** One of my complaints if you really want to know is that the recycling bins are not clearly labeled.

**17.** Which version is punctuated correctly?
    **a.** The childrens' books are located on the first floor.
    **b.** The children's books are located on the first floor.
    **c.** The childrens books are located on the first floor.
    **d.** The childrens's books are located on the first floor.

**18.** Which version is punctuated correctly?
    **a.** Whose laptop is this? Is it yours or Eric's?
    **b.** Whose laptop is this? Is it your's or Eric's?
    **c.** Who's laptop is this? Is it your's or Eric's?
    **d.** Who's laptop is this? Is it yours or Eric's?

**19.** Which version is punctuated correctly?
   **a.** "May I ride with you?" asked Del. "I can't get my car started."
   **b.** May I ride with you? asked Del. "I can't get my car started."
   **c.** "May I ride with you? asked Del. I can't get my car started."
   **d.** "May I ride with you"? asked Del, "I can't get my car started."

**20.** Which of the following items should be placed in quotations marks and should NOT be italicized or underlined?
   **a.** the title of a book
   **b.** the title of a story
   **c.** the title of a movie
   **d.** the title of a newspaper

**21.** Which version uses hyphens correctly?
   **a.** The well-known singer-songwriter gave a three hour concert.
   **b.** The well known singer songwriter gave a three-hour concert.
   **c.** The well-known singer-songwriter gave a three-hour concert.
   **d.** The well known singer-songwriter gave a three hour concert.

**22.** Which of the following should NOT be hyphenated?
   **a.** forty-five dollars
   **b.** one-hundredth of an inch
   **c.** a ten-minute break
   **d.** five-pieces of gum

**23.** Which version uses parentheses correctly?
    **a.** The company is looking into opening a branch in the Central American country of Belize (formerly known as British Honduras).
    **b.** The company is looking into opening a branch in (Central American country of) Belize, formerly known as British Honduras.
    **c.** The company is (looking) into opening a branch in the Central American country of Belize, formerly known as British Honduras.
    **d.** The company is looking into opening a branch in the Central American country (of Belize) formerly known as British Honduras.

For questions 24 and 25, choose the correct verb form.

**24.** Last night, Rita _____ a standing ovation for her keynote address.
    **a.** has gotten
    **b.** gotten
    **c.** will get
    **d.** got

**25.** Brandon _____ his camera so he could photograph the event.
    **a.** brang
    **b.** brought
    **c.** bring
    **d.** had brung

**26.** Which of the following underlined verbs is NOT written in the correct tense?

I **(a)** <u>look</u> forward to our meeting on December 20. Please **(b)** <u>bring</u> any examples of projects you **(c)** <u>worked</u> on in the past. We **(d)** <u>would meet</u> in my office on Peoria Street.

**a.** look
**b.** bring
**c.** worked
**d.** would meet

**27.** Which of the following sentences is in active voice?
   **a.** I was taken on a tour of the factory by the manager before I left.
   **b.** Before I left, I was taken on a tour of the factory by the manager.
   **c.** Before I left, the manager took me on a tour of the factory.
   **d.** I was taken on a tour of the factory before I left, by the manager.

**28.** Which of the following sentences is in the passive voice?
   **a.** Maya hoped that the reception would not be ruined by the impending thunderstorm.
   **b.** Maya was hoping that the reception would not be ruined by the impending thunderstorm.
   **c.** Maya is hoping that the reception won't be ruined by the impending thunderstorm.
   **d.** Maya has hoped that the reception won't be ruined by the impending thunderstorm.

For questions 29 and 30, choose the verb that agrees with the subject of the sentence.

**29.** Neither of the directors _____ to the regional meeting before.
   **a.** have been
   **b.** were
   **c.** is been
   **d.** has been

**30.** Christian and Jennifer _____ to find the perfect candidate to fill the position that is opening up.
   **a.** are trying
   **b.** is trying
   **c.** tried
   **d.** have tried

**31.** Choose the subject that agrees with the verb in the following sentence.

   _____ of the customers have complained about poor service.

   **a.** One
   **b.** Neither
   **c.** Each
   **d.** Some

**32.** In which of the following sentences is the underlined verb NOT in agreement with the subject of the sentence?
   **a.** Where <u>are</u> the forms you want me to fill out?
   **b.** Which <u>is</u> the correct form?
   **c.** Here <u>is</u> the forms you need to complete.
   **d.** There <u>are</u> two people who still need to complete the form.

**33.** In which of the following sentences is the underlined pronoun incorrect?

    **a.** Alicia and <u>me</u> want to spend Friday reviewing the website content.

    **b.** Either Sam or William will bring <u>his</u> car to the airport.

    **c.** She and <u>I</u> will work together on the project.

    **d.** Why not let <u>her</u> reschedule the meeting?

**34.** In which of the following sentences are the underlined pronouns correct?

    **a.** Would <u>he</u> or <u>me</u> be a better candidate?

    **b.** Would <u>he</u> or <u>I</u> be a better candidate?

    **c.** Would <u>him</u> or <u>me</u> be a better candidate?

    **d.** Would <u>him</u> or <u>I</u> be a better candidate?

For questions 35–38, choose the option that correctly completes the sentence.

**35.** Four team members and _____ were chosen to attend the state competition. One of _____ will do the driving.

    **a.** me, we

    **b.** me, us

    **c.** I, we

    **d.** I, us

**36.** Marcus _____ four reams of paper next to the copier earlier in the day.

    **a.** had sat

    **b.** set

    **c.** sit

    **d.** sat

**37.** About five minutes after the sun _____, our customers wake up, and _____ time to prepare for them.
   **a.** raises, it's
   **b.** raises, its
   **c.** rises, it's
   **d.** rises, its

**38.** Julian spoke _____ at the conference, but Kyle gave the _____ presentation I have ever seen.
   **a.** good, better
   **b.** good, best
   **c.** well, better
   **d.** well, best

**39.** Which of the sentences is clearly and correctly written?
   **a.** Driving along the country road, a deer ran in front of us.
   **b.** A deer ran in front of us while driving along the country road.
   **c.** As we were driving along the country road, a deer ran in front of us.
   **d.** Running in front of us, we saw the deer, driving along the country road.

For questions 40–46, choose the option that correctly completes the sentence.

**40.** If we divide this project _____ the five people here, there won't be _____ work left over.
   **a.** among, any
   **b.** among, no
   **c.** between, any
   **d.** between, no

**41.** Yesterday, I _____ some clients on a tour of our new distribution _____.
a. lead, cite
b. lead, site
c. led, cite
d. led, site

**42.** As we have done in the _____, we will _____ at the coffeehouse at 10:00 A.M.
a. past, meet
b. past, meat
c. passed, meet
d. passed, meat

**43.** As you can _____ see, there has been a _____ in the water pipe.
a. planely, brake
b. planely, break
c. plainly, brake
d. plainly, break

**44.** Do you know _____ Teresa will _____ to join our organization?
a. weather, choose
b. weather, chose
c. whether, choose
d. whether, chose

**45.** Did you _____ the badge you were supposed to _____ to get into the conference?
a. loose, wear
b. lose, where
c. loss, wear
d. lose, wear

**46.** Do you _____ if Serena Williams _____ the tournament?
    **a.** know, one
    **b.** know, won
    **c.** no, one
    **d.** no, won

**47.** Which of the following phrases contains a redundancy? (It expresses the same idea twice, with different words.)
    **a.** I did not go to the retail website.
    **b.** She always does very well in negotiations.
    **c.** The judges have temporarily delayed the competition until later.
    **d.** Liz and Lauren have both contributed greatly to the fundraising campaign.

**48.** Which of the following sentences contains a cliché?
    **a.** Why not start now? There's no time like the present.
    **b.** Just keep trying. You'll catch on.
    **c.** Whew! I'm tired.
    **d.** I'm as shocked at the news as you are.

**49.** Which version has a consistent point of view?
    **a.** The history of English is divided into three periods. You could mark the earliest one at about the fifth century A.D.
    **b.** You can say that the history of English could be divided into three periods, and I know the earliest one begins about the fifth century A.D.
    **c.** The history of English is divided into three periods. The earliest one begins at about the fifth century A.D.
    **d.** I learned that the history of English is divided into three periods and that you begin the earliest one at about the fifth century A.D.

**50.** Which version has a parallel structure?
    **a.** We write for a variety of purposes: in expressing our feelings, to convey information, to persuade, or to give pleasure.
    **b.** We write for a variety of purposes: to express our feelings, convey information, persuasion, or giving pleasure.
    **c.** We write for a variety of purposes: an expression of our feelings, conveying information, persuade, or to give pleasure.
    **d.** We write for a variety of purposes: to express our feelings, to convey information, to persuade, or to give pleasure.

# Answers

**1.** Choice **b** is correct. *Deputy* and *Judge* are being used as names, whereas *comissioner's assistant* is describing Ray; it's not part of his name.
Choice **a** is incorrect. *Deputy* should be capitalized because it is used as a name here.
Choice **c** is incorrect. *Judge* should be capitalized because it is being used as a name.
Choice **d** is incorrect. *Commissioner's Assistant* should not be capitalized because it is being used as an adjective to describe Ray.

**2.** Choice **b** is correct. The Fourth of July is a holiday, which makes the entire phrase a proper noun that should be capitalized.
Choice **a** is incorrect. Because *governor* is preceded by the article *the*, it is not a proper noun. Therefore, it should stay lowercase.
Choice **c** is incorrect. *Cousin* is not a proper noun unless it's a direct part of a name or title. It should not be capitalized here.
Choice **d** is incorrect. *East* is given as a direction here, not a specific geographical region, so it should not be capitalized in this sentence.

**3.** Choice **d** is correct. The war in question is a specific one: the Korean War. This should be capitalized as a proper noun.

Choice **a** is incorrect. *Spring* is not a proper noun and should not be capitalized.

Choice **b** is incorrect. *Network* is not a proper noun and should not be capitalized.

Choice **c** is incorrect. *History* is not a proper noun.

**4.** Choice **d** is correct. All abbreviations in this sentence except *IL* should be punctuated with a period.

Choice **a** is incorrect. The abbreviations *Dr.* (doctor), *Thurs.* (Thursday), and *P.M.* (*post meridiem*) should always be followed by a period.

Choice **b** is incorrect. State abbreviations like *IL* should not be followed by a period, but abbreviations for days of the week like *Thurs.* should be followed by a period.

Choice **c** is incorrect. State abbreviations like *IL* should not be followed by a period.

**5.** Choice **b** is correct. *Wow* is an exclamation and is punctuated correctly with an exclamation point. *That was a successful novel* is a statement, so the period is correct. And *What other books has this author written* is a question, so the question mark is correct.

Choice **a** is incorrect. The first sentence, *Wow, that was a successful novel*, is a statement, not a question, and should not end with a question mark. The second sentence is a question, not an exclamatory statement, and should end with a question mark instead of an exclamation point.

Choice **c** is incorrect. *Wow* is an exclamation, not a question, so it should end with an exclamation point.

Choice **d** is incorrect. *Wow* is an exclamation, not a statement, so it should end with an exclamation point. Also, *That was a successful novel* is a statement, not a question, and should end with a period instead of a question mark.

**6.** Choice **c** is correct. *Sunday afternoon spent preparing for Monday's big meeting* is not a complete sentence. It is missing a verb and does not express a complete thought: *Who* spent Sunday afternoon preparing? Sunday afternoon spent preparing *what*? The information is incomplete, and so this is a sentence fragment.

Choice **a** is incorrect. *Hearing the thunder* is a fragment, but it is followed by a complete sentence (*the lifeguard ordered the swimmers out of the water*). Therefore, it is an independent clause and not a fragment.

Choice **b** is incorrect. *Turn off the printer* is an order directed at the listener (an implied *you*), so it is considered a complete sentence.

Choice **d** is incorrect. This choice contains all the necessary elements of a sentence: subjects (*I* and *our C.E.O.*), verbs (*was* and *had written*), and a complete thought.

**7.** Choice **a** is correct. This choice contains two complete thoughts, joined by the conjunction *but*. Therefore, it is a compound sentence, not a faulty one.

Choice **b** is incorrect. *I called the caterers this morning* is a complete sentence, as is *they told me lunch would arrive on time*. However, there is no coordinating conjunction to connect the two thoughts, so this choice is a comma splice.

Choice **c** is incorrect. There is no punctuation to tell you where one statement ends and the other begins, which makes this a run-on sentence.

Choice **d** is incorrect. *I was the first to sign the petition* is a complete thought, and *Harry was second* is another. However, because there is no separation between the two thoughts, this is a run-on sentence.

**8.** Choice **d** is correct. The subordinate clause is correctly set off by commas, and *year's* has the correct apostrophe.

Choice **a** is incorrect. There should be a comma after *year* to set off the subordinate clause *who ran in the Boston*

*Marathon last year.* Additionally, there should be an apostrophe in *year's* because it is possessive.

Choice **b** is incorrect. There should be a comma after *Charlotte* to set off the subordinate clause *who ran in the Boston Marathon last year.* Also, the comma after *Boston Marathon* should not be there.

Choice **c** is incorrect. There should be a comma after *Charlotte* to set off the subordinate clause *who ran in the Boston Marathon last year.*

9. Choice **b** is correct. *Who does not have a camping permit* is a restrictive clause (meaning it offers essential information), so it should not be set off with commas. The sentence is punctuated correctly.

Choice **a** is incorrect. *Who does not have a camping permit* is a restrictive clause (meaning it offers essential information), so it should not be set off with commas.

Choice **c** is incorrect. The comma after the word *anyone* is incorrect and confusing—it doesn't set off a subordinate clause, and it separates the information into two disjointed parts.

Choice **d** is incorrect. The comma after *permit* incorrectly separates the sentence into two parts without indicating a clause or forming any particular order.

10. Choice **a** is correct. The commas in this sentence group the clauses correctly: *As soon as she finished her dinner* is the introductory clause, *who is a volunteer at the hospital* is a nonrestrictive clause, and *Lisa . . . reported for her shift* is the independent clause that holds the sentence together.

Choice **b** is incorrect. Because *who is a volunteer at the hospital* is a nonrestrictive clause (it offers extra information about Lisa that is not essential to the sentence), a comma is needed after *hospital* to set it off.

Choice **c** is incorrect. *Her dinner* is not a clause on its own and should not be set off by commas.

Choice **d** is incorrect. Because *who is a volunteer at the hospital* is a nonrestrictive clause (it offers extra information about Lisa that is not essential to the sentence), commas are needed after *Lisa* and after *hospital* to set it off.

**11.** Choice **d** is correct. When punctuating a street address, you should always use a comma after the street address and after the town name.

Choice **a** is incorrect. Although a date should always have a comma after the day (*December 15,*), it is not essential to have a comma after the year unless the date is part of a subordinate clause.

Choice **b** is incorrect. Using a comma instead of a semicolon or a period here creates a run-on sentence.

Choice **c** is incorrect. *When she was five* is a restrictive, or essential, clause that tells you when Ms. Sym moved, relative to her birth date. Therefore, it shouldn't be set off with a comma.

**12.** Choice **d** is correct. *Yes* is an introductory clause and should be followed by a comma. This is a compound sentence: *I would like to review the loan application* is the first independent clause, and *Please send it as soon as you can* is the second independent clause. The comma should come before the coordinating conjunction (*and*) that connects the sentence's two independent clauses.

Choice **a** is incorrect. With no punctuation at all, this is a run-on sentence.

Choice **b** is incorrect. *And* is used as a coordinating conjunction connecting the sentence's two independent clauses. The comma should come before the coordinating conjunction, not after *it*.

Choice **c** is incorrect. *And* is used as a coordinating conjunction connecting the sentence's two independent clauses. The comma should come before the coordinating conjunction.

**13.** Choice **a** is correct. The independent clause (*It seems . . . your shipment has been delayed*) surrounds an appositive (*Mr. May*). This appositive is set off by commas because it is restating the name of *you*, the person to whom the speaker is addressing. *We apologize for any inconvenience* is correctly separated as its own sentence.

Choice **b** is incorrect. Without commas, semicolons, periods, or anything else separating the parts of the sentence, the meaning is difficult to figure out. This is a run-on sentence.

Choice **c** is incorrect. While *Mr. May* is correctly set off with commas, the comma after *delayed* turns the sentence into a comma splice (two independent clauses joined by a comma).

Choice **d** is incorrect. The sentences are correctly split into two, but the appositive *Mr. May* should be set off by commas because it is restating the name of *you*, the person to whom the speaker is addressing.

**14.** Choice **c** is correct. The semicolon divides the independent clauses into separate (but related) thoughts without needing a conjunction. Because *therefore* becomes an introductory word after the semicolon, it is correctly punctuated with a comma.

Choice **a** is incorrect. A comma between *tonight* and *therefore* (without a coordinating conjunction) creates a comma splice because both parts of the sentence are independent clauses.

Choice **b** is incorrect. A comma between *tonight* and *therefore* (without a coordinating conjunction) creates a comma splice because both parts of the sentence are independent clauses.

Choice **d** is incorrect. The semicolon and the comma are switched.

**15.** Choice **b** is correct. *Any of the following* lets you know that a list is coming, and a colon is the correct punctuation mark to introduce a list.

Choice **a** is incorrect. A comma is not the correct punctuation mark to introduce a list and leaves the list without definition.

Choice **c** is incorrect. A semicolon is used to separate independent thoughts and is not the correct punctuation mark to introduce a list.

Choice **d** is incorrect. The list of organizations is not a sentence on its own; using a period after *organizations* is incorrect.

**16.** Choice **b** is correct. The em-dashes are used to set off the author's own comment (*if you really want to know*) because (1) the author is pausing to add this aside; and (2) the information contained in the clause is not essential to the meaning of the sentence.

Choice **a** is incorrect. The em-dash (—) is used for emphasis, as well as for separating nonrestrictive clauses. The punctuation should be consistent within a sentence. If you start a clause off with an em-dash, you should end it with an em-dash as well.

Choice **c** is incorrect. The punctuation should be consistent within a sentence. If you start a clause with an em-dash, you should end it with an em-dash as well.

Choice **d** is incorrect. The absence of punctuation makes this sentence difficult to understand. The author's comment (*if you really want to know*) should be set off with em-dashes.

**17.** Choice **b** is correct. *Children's* is the possessive of *children* and indicates who the books belong to.

Choice **a** is incorrect. The books belong to the *children*, so the apostrophe belongs between the *n* and *s*.

Choice **c** is incorrect. *Childrens* requires an apostrophe to indicate who the books belong to.

Choice **d** is incorrect. The possessive of *children* is *children's*.

**18.** Choice **a** is correct. *Whose* and *yours* are possessive pronouns, so no apostrophe is needed in either case. *Eric's* is possessive, so it should have an apostrophe.

Choice **b** is incorrect. *Yours* should never have an apostrophe. Possessive pronouns do not require apostrophes, even when they are plural.

Choice **c** is incorrect. The possessive pronoun of *who* is *whose*, not *who's*, and *yours* should never have an apostrophe. Possessive pronouns do not require apostrophes, even when they are plural.

Choice **d** is incorrect. The possessive pronoun of *who* is *whose*, not *who's*. However, possessive versions of names (like *Eric*) should always have an apostrophe (*Eric's*).

**19.** Choice **a** is correct. Del's two direct quotes should be punctuated with quotation marks.

Choice **b** is incorrect. Without quotation marks, the reader can't tell that *May I ride with you?* is a direct quote from Del.

Choice **c** is incorrect. *Asked Del* is a tag that tells you who is speaking; it is not part of the quotation. You should be careful to make sure that each part of the quote has the necessary opening and closing quotation marks.

Choice **d** is incorrect. The question mark is part of Del's quote, so it should be included inside the ending quotation mark.

**20.** Choice **b** is correct. Stories and other smaller parts of a larger work should be placed in quotation marks.

Choice **a** is incorrect. A book is considered a complete work in itself, so it should be italicized or underlined.

Choice **c** is incorrect. A movie is considered a complete work in itself, so it should be italicized or underlined.

Choice **d** is incorrect. A newspaper is a larger work containing smaller pieces (articles), so it should be italicized or underlined.

**21.** Choice **c** is correct. The adjective phrase, the coequal nouns, and the number-word adjective phrase should all be hyphenated.

Choice **a** is incorrect. *Well-known* and *singer-songwriter* are hyphenated correctly, but *three-hour* should also have a hyphen because it is a number-word adjective.

Choice **b** is incorrect. *Well* and *known* work together as a single adjective, and because the adjective phrase comes before the noun, it should contain a hyphen. Additionally, *singer* and *songwriter* should be hyphenated because they are coequal nouns working together to describe a single person.

Choice **d** is incorrect. The adjective phrase *well-known* should be hyphenated because the words work together as a single adjective and come before the noun they modify. The number-word adjective *three-hour* should also be hyphenated.

**22.** Choice **d** is correct. *Five* and *pieces* are separate words and not joined together as an adjective. Therefore, they should not be connected with a hyphen.

Choice **a** is incorrect. All numbers between 21 and 99 should contain hyphens when they're written as words.

Choice **b** is incorrect. Fractions that are written as words should be hyphenated.

Choice **c** is incorrect. Number-word adjective phrases should always contain hyphens.

**23.** Choice **a** is correct. The parentheses are used to set off additional information (the former name of Belize) that is not necessary to the sentence's meaning.

Choice **b** is incorrect. *Central American country of* does not interrupt the sentence, and if it were removed, crucial information about where the country is located would be missing.

Choice **c** is incorrect. The information inside the parentheses is not extra information, and if it were removed, you wouldn't be able to tell what the company is doing.

Choice **d** is incorrect. The information inside the parentheses is not extra information, and if it were removed, you would not know which country the company is looking into opening a branch in.

**24.** Choice **d** is correct. *Got* is the past tense of *to get*, and because the event happened last night (and is not still happening), a past tense is correct.

Choice **a** is incorrect. *Last night* tells you that the event is in the past. *Has gotten* is the present-perfect tense.

Choice **b** is incorrect. *Gotten* is the past participle of *to get*, but it is not correct here because past participles should always be preceded by *has/have/had*.

Choice **c** is incorrect. *Last night* tells you that the event is in the past, but *will get* is future tense.

**25.** Choice **b** is correct. *So he could photograph the event* is the past tense, so this tells you that you are looking for another past-tense verb for consistency. *Brought* is the correct past-tense form of the verb *to bring*.

Choice **a** is incorrect. *Brang* is not a word.

Choice **c** is incorrect. Because *so he could photograph the event* is in the past tense, the simple-perfect tense (*bring*) does not fit in this sentence.

Choice **d** is incorrect. *Brung* is not a word, and *had brung* is not a correct form of the verb *to bring*.

**26.** Choice **d** is correct. Because the paragraph is discussing an event that is happening in the future, this sentence requires the future tense: *will meet*.

Choice **a** is incorrect. *Look* indicates that the author is currently anticipating the meeting.

Choice **b** is incorrect. The verb *bring* is in the correct tense.

Choice **c** is incorrect. *Worked* is the correct past tense.

**27.** Choice **c** is correct. *The manager took me on a tour of the factory* is written in the active voice—the manager is performing the action directly.

Choice **a** is incorrect. *I was taken* is written in the passive voice.

Choice **b** is incorrect. *I was taken* is written in the passive voice.

Choice **d** is incorrect. *I was taken* is written in the passive voice.

**28.** Choice **b** is correct. *Maya was hoping* contains a passive verb phrase because there is an additional verb separating the subject (*Maya*) and the active verb (*hoping*).

Choice **a** is incorrect. *Maya hoped* contains an active verb phrase, not a passive verb phrase.

Choice **c** is incorrect. *Maya is hoping* contains a future-tense verb, not a passive verb phrase.

Choice **d** is incorrect. *Maya has hoped* contains a past-perfect-tense verb, not a passive verb phrase.

**29.** Choice **d** is correct. *Has been* is a singular verb and agrees with the singular pronoun *neither*, which is the subject of the sentence.

Choice **a** is incorrect. *Have been* suggests that the subjects are plural; and although *directors* is plural, *neither* is the subject of the sentence and is a singular pronoun, which means that the sentence talks about the directors individually.

Choice **b** is incorrect. This choice is missing the past participle. The directors *were* doing what? This choice leaves you hanging. It also suggests a plural subject, which doesn't match the actual, singular subject (*neither*).

Choice **c** is incorrect. *Is been* is not a correct form of the verb *to be*, so it cannot be correct in this sentence.

**30.** Choice **a** is correct. *Christian and Jennifer* is a plural subject, so *are* is correct (*that is opening up* indicates that the event will happen in the future, but they *are trying* now, so the present form of the verb is needed).

Choice **b** is incorrect. *Is* is singular, but *Christian and Jennifer* is a plural subject.

Choice **c** is incorrect. Because you know that the event has not yet taken place (the phrase *that is opening up* indicates that the event will happen in the future), the past-tense verb *tried* can be eliminated.

Choice **d** is incorrect. Because the phrase *that is opening up* indicates that the event has not yet taken place, the past-tense verb *have tried* can be eliminated.

**31.** Choice **d** is correct. *Some* means more than one customer, which agrees with the plural verb *have complained*.

Choice **a** is incorrect. The verb *have complained* suggests that the number of customers is plural, so the singular pronoun *one* cannot be correct.

Choice **b** is incorrect. The verb *have complained* suggests that the number of customers is plural, so the singular pronoun *neither* cannot be correct.

Choice **c** is incorrect. The verb *have complained* suggests that the number of customers is plural, so the singular pronoun *each* cannot be correct.

**32.** Choice **c** is correct. The verb *is* is singular, and it does not agree with the plural subject *forms*.

Choice **a** is incorrect. *Are* agrees with the plural *forms*.

Choice **b** is incorrect. The verb *is* agrees with the singular *form*.

Choice **d** is incorrect. The verb *are* agrees with the plural *people*.

**33.** Choice **a** is correct. The underlined pronoun is acting as the subject of the sentence along with Alicia, so the nominative case pronoun *I* is needed.

Choice **b** is incorrect. The conjunction *either . . . or* treats Sam and William separately, and therefore singularly, so the singular pronoun *his* is correct.

Choice **c** is incorrect. *I* is used correctly as a nominative-case pronoun in the subject of the sentence, naming the speaker along with *she*.

Choice **d** is incorrect. *Her* is the correct objective-case pronoun because it follows the action verb *let*.

**34.** Choice **b** is correct. Both *he* and *I* are the correct nominative-case pronouns in the subject of this sentence.

Choice **a** is incorrect. *He* is the correct nominative-case pronoun, but *me* is an objective-case pronoun. Because these make up the subject of the sentence, both pronouns need to be in the nominative case. *Me* should be *I*.

Choice **c** is incorrect. *Him* and *me* are objective-case pronouns, but they are acting as the subjects of the sentence. Pronouns that act as subjects must be in the nominative case.

Choice **d** is incorrect. *Him* is objective and *I* is nominative. Because these make up the subject of the sentence, both pronouns need to be in the nominative case.

**35.** Choice **d** is correct. The nominative-case pronoun *I* and the objective-case pronoun *us* are used correctly in this sentence.

Choice **a** is incorrect. *Me* is an objective-case pronoun, but in this sentence it is acting as the subject, which requires a nominative-case pronoun. Also, *we* is a nominative-case pronoun, but in this sentence it is the object of the preposition *of*, which requires an objective-case pronoun.

Choice **b** is incorrect. *Me* is an objective-case pronoun, but in this sentence it is acting as the subject, which requires a nominative-case pronoun.

Choice **c** is incorrect. In the second sentence, *we* is a nominative-case pronoun, but in this sentence it is the object of the preposition *of*, which requires an objective-case pronoun.

**36.** Choice **b** is correct. *Set*, which means *to put* or *to place*, is the most accurate description of Marcus leaving the reams of paper by the copier.

Choice **a** is incorrect. In sentences like this, you should look at the meanings of the words you're filling in. *Sat* means *rested*; is that the meaning you want? *Set*, which means *to put* or *to place*, is a more accurate description of Marcus leaving the reams of paper by the copier. *Rested* is close, but would you normally say that he *rested* something next to the copier, or that he *put* something next to the copier?

Choice **c** is incorrect. *Sit* is a present-tense verb, while the sentence reveals that the action took place in the past. A past-tense verb is needed.

Choice **d** is incorrect. In sentences like this, you should look at the meanings of the words you're filling in. *Sat* means *rested*; is that the meaning you want? *Set*, which means *to put* or *to place*, is a more accurate description of Marcus leaving the paper near the copier. *Rested* is close, but would you normally say that he *rested* something near the copier, or that he *put* something near the copier?

**37.** Choice **c** is correct. Both the word choice (*rises*) and the contraction *it's* are correct.

Choice **a** is incorrect. Because *raise* is a verb easily confused with *rise*, you need to look closely at the word's meaning. To *raise* means to *move up*. Does the sun *move up*, or does it *go up*? In this case, *rise* is the more accurate option.

Choice **b** is incorrect. Because *raise* is a verb easily confused with *rise*, you need to look closely at the word's meaning. To *raise* means to *move up*. Does the sun *move up*, or does it *go up*? In this case, *rise* is the more accurate option. Additionally, the possessive pronoun *its* is incorrect in this sentence. *Its* should be *it's*, the contraction of *it is*.

Choice **d** is incorrect. Additionally, the possessive pronoun *its* is incorrect in this sentence. *Its* should be *it's*, the contraction of *it is*.

**38.** Choice **d** is correct. The adverb w*ell* modifies *spoke*, and the superlative modifier *best* tells you how Kyle's presentation compares to Julian's and any others who aren't mentioned by name.

Choice **a** is incorrect. In the first blank, you're seeking a word to modify the verb *spoke*—in other words, an adverb. *Good* is an adjective, so you can eliminate this choice. Also, *better* is a comparative adverb that compares two items. However, the *ever seen* suggests that there were more presentations than Kyle's and Julian's, so you need a different modifier that compares more than two. In this case, that would be the superlative adverb, *best*.

Choice **b** is incorrect. In the first blank, you're seeking a word to modify the verb *spoke*—in other words, an adverb. *Good* is an adjective, so you can eliminate this choice.

Choice **c** is incorrect. *Well* is an adverb that correctly modifies the verb *spoke*. *Better* is a comparative adverb that compares two items, but the phrase *ever seen* suggests that there were more presentations than Kyle's and Julian's. A different modifier is needed that compares more than two presentations. In this case, that would be the superlative adverb, *best*.

**39.** Choice **c** is correct. In the introductory clause it is clear that *we* are driving the car. The pause at the comma lets you know that the two ideas are separate (that we were driving the car AND that the deer ran across the road in front of the car). This sentence is the clearest of the choices.

Choice **a** is incorrect. Because *a deer* directly follows *Driving along the country road*, it sounds like the deer is driving the car. This is an amusing image, but it makes for an incorrect and unclear sentence.

Choice **b** is incorrect. The way this sentence is written, it's unclear who is driving the car. Any scenario that could end with the deer driving the car should be eliminated as an incorrect sentence.

Choice **d** is incorrect. This sentence manages to make it sound like the people are running and the deer is driving. It is very unclear and needs to be rewritten.

**40.** Choice **a** is correct. *Among* means that more than two people will be involved; the sentence tells you that there are five people. For the second blank, look at the clues around the blank: *there won't be . . . work left over.* You know there will be no work left, but hopefully you also noticed that the sentence already contains *won't.* Another negative word like *no* would create a double negative, which indicates that *any* is correct.

Choice **b** is incorrect. *Among* matches *five people*, but *no* creates a double negative with *won't.*

Choice **c** is incorrect. The preposition *between* is incorrect because it divides into two, and you already know from the sentence that you're dealing with five people.

Choice **d** is incorrect. The preposition *between* is incorrect because it divides into two, and you already know from the sentence that you're dealing with five people. Also, the word *no* creates an incorrect double negative with *won't.*

**41.** Choice **d** is correct. The sentence tells you that the action took place yesterday, so the past-tense verb *led* is correct. Also, *site* refers to a physical location and has the correct meaning in this sentence: *I led some clients on a tour of our new distribution [place].*

Choice **a** is incorrect. *Lead* is the simple present tense of the verb. However, the sentence tells you that the action took place yesterday, so the present tense is incorrect. For *cite/site,* you should look at the meaning of each word and determine which fits best. *Cite* means to refer to something, while *site* refers to a physical location. In the context of this sentence, *cite* is not the correct word because it does not have the correct meaning.

Choice **b** is incorrect. *Lead* is the simple present tense of the verb. However, the sentence tells you that the action took place yesterday, so the present tense is incorrect.

Choice **c** is incorrect. The past-tense *led* is correct. However, *cite* means to refer to something, while *site* refers to a physical location. In the context of this sentence, *cite* does not have the correct meaning.

**42.** Choice **a** is correct. The noun *past* completes the prepositional phrase; and the verb *meet* creates the action in the sentence.

Choice **b** is incorrect. Look closely at the sentence. *Meat* means flesh. Does it make sense that you will "[flesh] at the coffeehouse at 10:00 A.M."? *Meat* is a noun, but you need a verb to complete the sentence.

Choice **c** is incorrect. *In the* _____ is a prepositional phrase, so you're looking for a noun to fill in the blank as the object of the preposition. *Passed* is a verb, so it is incorrect here.

Choice **d** is incorrect. *Passed* is a verb, not a noun, so it cannot complete the prepositional phrase. Also, *meat* is a noun, but a verb is needed to complete the sentence.

**43.** Choice **d** is correct. *Plainly* is the correct adverb to modify *see*, and a *break* (or disruption) in the pipe sounds more realistic than a *brake* (or a device/object) in the pipe.

Choice **a** is incorrect. *Planely* is not a real word, and without a valid definition, you can't tell how the word should fit into the sentence. Also, if you think about the meaning of the word *brake*, the word doesn't seem to fit into the sentence either: . . . *there has been a [device for slowing] in the water pipe.*

Choice **b** is incorrect. *Planely* is not a real word, and without a valid definition, you can't tell how the word should fit into the sentence. *Break*, when used as a noun, means *a disruption*. This is the correct meaning for this sentence.

Choice **c** is incorrect. The adverb *plainly* (or obviously) has the correct meaning for this sentence. However, if you think about the meaning of *brake*, the word doesn't fit into the sentence: . . . *there has been a [device for slowing] in the water pipe.*

**44.** Choice **c** is correct. The conjunction *whether* works with the verb *to choose* (it sets up Teresa's alternatives of choosing the organization or not choosing the organization), and the future tense of *choose* aligns with *Teresa will.*

Choice **a** is incorrect. This is another question where you should look at the definitions of two easily confused words. *Weather*, a noun, is an atmospheric state. *Whether*, a conjunction, is meant to introduce alternatives. In the context of this sentence, the conjunction *whether* has the correct meaning.

Choice **b** is incorrect. In addition to *weather* not having the correct meaning for this sentence, *chose* is incorrect. The sentence is in future tense (*Teresa will*), so the past-tense verb *chose* is not consistent with the rest of the sentence.

Choice **d** is incorrect. This usage of *whether* is correct, but the past-tense verb *chose* is not consistent with the rest of the sentence in future tense.

**45.** Choice **d** is correct. When you read the sentence, you can see that you need a verb in each blank. *Lose* is a verb, and so is *wear*; both have the correct meanings to complete this sentence.

Choice **a** is incorrect. *Loose* is either an adjective that means *free* or *not tight*, or a verb that means *to set free*. In this sentence, you need a verb that goes with the subject, *badge*. It is not likely that you'd be setting a badge free, so you should look for another verb that better fits the meaning of the sentence.

Choice **b** is incorrect. The verb *lose* is correct in this sentence ("Did you [fail to keep] the badge?"), but the second part of the sentence calls for a verb as well. *Where* is an adverb that describes place.

Choice **c** is incorrect. *Loss* is a noun, while you already know from reading the sentence that you need a verb. However, *wear* is the correct verb form of the easily confused word in the second blank.

**46.** Choice **b** is correct. Both *know* and *won* are verbs. When you insert them into the sentence, the thought is complete and makes sense: *Do you know if Serena Williams won the tournament?*

Choice **a** is incorrect. From the context of the sentence, you can tell that you need a verb (alongside the subject *you*) and then another verb (what act did Serena Williams perform?). *Know* is a verb, but *one* is a noun, making it an incorrect choice for the second blank.

Choice **c** is incorrect. *No* is a versatile word that can be several different parts of speech (noun, adverb, adjective), but it is never a verb. *One* is also not a verb; it's a noun meaning *single*. Neither word fits the sentence.

Choice **d** is incorrect. *No* is a versatile word that can be several different parts of speech (noun, adverb, adjective), but it is never a verb. *Won* is a verb and has the correct meaning to complete this sentence.

**47.** Choice **c** is correct. When you see the words *temporarily delayed*, you can already infer that the judges have postponed the competition to a future date. Therefore, *until later* at the end of the sentence repeats information you already know and is therefore redundant.

Choice **a** is incorrect. This sentence is straightforward; nothing is repeated.

Choice **b** is incorrect. This sentence does have two modifiers that describe *well* (*very* and *in negotiations*), but they do not compete by expressing the same idea.

Choice **d** is incorrect. Because you see two subjects (Liz and Lauren) as well as the word *both*, you might assume that this is redundant. However, *both* is an important compound pronoun that tells you that each woman performed the action in the sentence and is not redundant.

**48.** Choice **a** is correct. "There's no time like the present" is an exact phrase you've undoubtedly heard hundreds (if not thousands!) of times in your life. If you read or hear a sentence that automatically sounds like you've heard it before in that exact form, it is very likely a cliché.

Choice **b** is incorrect. *Just keep trying* may be a common idea, but as a specific phrase it isn't necessarily a cliché. The idea may be a cliché, but this particular phrase is not.

Choice **c** is incorrect. This sentence is a statement of how the speaker is feeling. Again, this might be a common feeling or sentiment, but a cliché is a specific phrase that has been used over and over.

Choice **d** is incorrect. This sentence is more of a statement of a common feeling than a specific phrase or sentence that you've heard before.

**49.** Choice **c** is correct. Both the first and second sentences are told in the third person.

Choice **a** is incorrect. This choice starts with a third-person narration (*The history of English is . . .*), then moves into the second person (*You could mark . . .*).

Choice **b** is incorrect. This choice starts with the second person (*You can say that . . .*), but then switches over to the first person (*I know the . . .*).

Choice **d** is incorrect. The first person (*I learned that . . .*) quickly shifts to the second person (*you begin . . .*) in the same sentence.

**50.** Choice **d** is correct. The colon after *We write for a variety of purposes* tells you that you're reading a list. Each item in the list starts with the infinitive phrase *to + verb*, making each item parallel to the others.

Choice **a** is incorrect. The colon after *We write for a variety of purposes* tells you that you're reading a list. If the list were parallel, all items would be presented in the same way. *In expressing our feelings* is not an infinitive phrase that uses *to*, like the other list items are.

Choice **b** is incorrect. The list starts with the infinitive preposition *to*, but then each list item is written in a different way: simple verb phrase (*convey information*), noun (*persuasion*), and transitive verb phrase (*giving pleasure*).

Choice **c** is incorrect. If the list were parallel, all items would be presented in the same way, but each list item is written in a different way: a noun (*an expression of our feelings*), a transitive verb (*conveying information*), and an infinitive phrase (*to give pleasure*).

# Section 1: Writing to Get the Job You Want

**W**hether you're using this book as you enter the professional workforce for the first time, as you return to it after an absence, as you change careers, or just to improve your performance, these job-seeking and workplace tips will help you make an exemplary first impression. Begin by drafting knockout resumes and cover letters, then prepare for interviews like a pro, and find out exactly what to expect as you start your new job. Your first impression begins the moment your resume hits your future employer's inbox, and a little planning ahead will help you stand out.

# 1 Writing Resumes and Cover Letters

**J**ob hunting is stressful under the best of circumstances—preparing exemplary resumes and cover letters is a great way to feel prepared and to make the most out of your first impression.

Once you've crafted a resume that represents you at your most professionally appealing, you may want to consider creating a LinkedIn page to help you share your job-hunting materials with members of your professional and social networks.

## ↪ RESUME TIPS

- Create multiple versions of your resume and adapt your experience for each position as you apply.

- Be brief and stay focused when writing about your work history and qualifications.

- Highlight your accomplishments as well as your responsibilities from each job.

- Use keywords that match specific job and industry requirements to help you get noticed.

- Use powerful action words and phrases to stand out from the competition.

- Make your resume viewable by posting it on LinkedIn and other networking sites.

- Always proofread and spell-check your resume before sending it out. Have a friend glance over it too—software won't catch homonyms or commonly confused words.

## What to Include in Your Resume

| | |
|---|---|
| Name | Skills |
| Contact info | Licenses/Certifications |
| Highlights of your qualifications | Honors/Awards |
| Experience | Publications/Presentations |
| Education | Professional Memberships |

## Name

Use your full name, no nicknames. If you have a relatively common name, consider adding your middle initial to distinguish yourself from the rest of the Jane Millers in the world.

## Contact Info

Leave your prospective employers with all the information they'll need to find you—address, phone number, and a professional-looking email address. Now is the time to abandon any SurferChick@ yahoo.com or Dougie134@hotmail.com addresses that have stuck with you since high school. Gmail and other providers offer free email addresses—see if YourFirstname.YourLastname@gmail.com is available (you can even set up your account to send and receive mail from your old addresses!) and check it regularly.

Make sure that each phone number you list will be answered, either by a person or a recorded message, 24 hours a day. If a potential employer calls, it is imperative that he or she be able to reach you on the first attempt.

## Highlights of your Qualifications

Briefly describe your work experience, talents, and accomplishments. Use strong action words and be sure to answer the question, "What can I do for an employer?"

If you're changing industries or careers, use this section to highlight accomplishments and qualifications that can be transferred to new job objectives. Make a list of what you have to offer and connect these traits, skills, and experiences to what the job description is seeking. You may also choose to include accomplishments that relate to unpaid positions but are relevant to a new industry. For example, if you're moving from an insurance company to a non-profit organization, highlights of a volunteer position might be included here.

## *Experience*

List your work experience in reverse chronological order. Resumes are read quickly, so focus on your best skills, your most relevant accomplishments, and the positive results of your work. Three to five bullets for any job description is a good target—remember that a resume is not your life story. Use strong action words throughout, and leave out unimportant information.

## *Education*

List your most recent degrees first. Don't abbreviate school names, regardless of how well known they are. Graduation dates are optional. You may choose to leave your dates off, but readers may assume that you're older than you are or that you never graduated.

If you attended college but didn't earn a degree, include start and end dates but don't list a degree name. If you're in the process of earning a degree, list the expected date of completion, as follows: "Expected May 2016." If you have an undergraduate degree or higher, there is no need to list your high school diploma or GED.

You may also include other relevant continuing education or completed classes—including class names, organizations or schools, cities and states, and key dates. If you have earned a significant certification, you may want to highlight it in a Licenses/Certifications section.

## *Skills*

In this section, list skills that are relevant to the job you're applying for, such as proficiency with a certain technology or special equipment or fluency in a foreign language.

For example:

- In-depth knowledge of AutoCAD, Excel, Word, and PowerPoint

- Fluent in Spanish
- Proficient in Microsoft Office applications and proprietary database maintenance
- ICD-9-CM and CPT Coding Expert, 2012

## Licenses/Certifications

Place certification and licensure information where it will be most effective on your resume.

If you're applying for a teaching job, include your certification information under **Education**. If you passed the bar exam, you might want this information under **Highlights of Qualifications**. If you're in the process of earning a professional license or certification, include that in the **Additional Information** section, along with the expected completion date.

## Honors/Awards

If you have significant honors or awards that you wish to highlight, list them here in reverse chronological order. Honors or awards that aren't professional or academic should only be listed if they are relevant to the job you're applying for. Do not include honors or awards that may be considered controversial.

Consider including awards in other resume sections if you have only one or two items to list. An award from an employer could easily be highlighted in a job description. An award from your college or university could be listed under **Education**.

## Publications/Presentations

List any notable publications or presentations, especially if relevant to the position for which you're applying. Display this information in reverse chronological order and include the complete title and all key details, such as issue/volume number, page numbers, and date. If part of a series, indicate the name of the series.

It is perfectly acceptable to list publications or presentations in other resume sections where this information might fit, such as in the **Experience** section as a bullet point describing a position.

You may also choose to include publications or presentations under **Additional Information** at the end of the resume. Only mention your publications or presentations once, though.

If you do not have any noteworthy publications or presentations, skip this section.

### Professional Memberships

List any relevant professional groups or associations, including your titles, locations, and membership dates. This is also a good place to highlight leadership roles.

### Formatting

Your resume should have tidy margins, normal fonts (avoid ornate scripts or anything cutesy like Comic Sans), and a balanced use of space. You don't want to give prospective employers eyestrain, nor do you want them to hunt for your qualifications on a too-blank page.

## Sample Keywords

Unless you're handing your resume directly to the person who makes hiring decisions (which is a great networking technique—if you know someone who knows someone, make the best use of that you can!), most companies use keyword-hunting software to sort through dozens of applications to find the ones with relevant experience. Prepare for this process by mining the job posting to see exactly what the company is seeking. Here's a sample list of qualifications:

- 1–2 years of experience preferred
- Financial services experience or knowledge preferred, but not required
- Exceptional verbal communication and written communication skills
- Self-motivated, with high energy and an engaging level of enthusiasm
- Able to work outside of normal business hours on event days as needed
- Professional personality, go-getter attitude
- Proactive, self-sufficient, and self-motivated
- Ability to prioritize and manage project timelines in a fast-paced environment
- Bachelor's degree required

If you were applying for this position, you would want to emphasize your *energetic attitude*, *excellent communication skills*, *multi-tasking abilities*, and *financial services experience* throughout your job experience descriptions.

## Compelling Action Verbs

An effective resume always includes action verbs that describe all the amazing things you *have done* in your previous jobs and what you *will do* in your desired position. If you're stuck coming up with compelling language, take a look at the following lists (sorted by industry type) to help make your descriptions engaging and dynamic.

## Creative Skills

Acclimated
Accomplished
Achieved
Acquired
Acted
Activated
Actuated
Adapted
Adopted
Affected
Altered
Amended
Anticipated
Began
Challenged
Changed
Chose
Combined
Completed
Composed
Conceived
Conceptualized
Condensed
Contrasted
Contrived
Crafted
Created

Customized
Designed
Developed
Devised
Directed
Displayed
Distinguished
Drew
Earned
Employed
Entertained
Established
Exercised
Fashioned
Forged
Formed
Formulated
Founded
Illustrated
Imagined
Improvised
Inaugurated
Induced
Initiated
Innovated
Instigated
Instituted

Integrated
Introduced
Invented
Isolated
Masterminded
Modeled
Modified
Named
Opened
Originated
Perceived
Performed
Photographed
Planned
Published
Reached
Realized
Rendered
Resulted
Revised
Revitalized
Shaped
Solved
Staged
Strategized
Tailored

## Data/Financial Skills

| | | |
|---|---|---|
| Added | Developed | Prepared |
| Adjusted | Discounted | Priced |
| Administered | Divested | Programmed |
| Allocated | Entered | Projected |
| Analyzed | Estimated | Prospected |
| Appraised | Exchanged | Qualified |
| Assessed | Exempted | Quantified |
| Audited | Extrapolated | Quoted |
| Balanced | Figured | Reconciled |
| Billed | Financed | Reduced |
| Bought | Forecasted | Researched |
| Borrowed | Gauged | Retrieved |
| Budgeted | Grossed | Saved |
| Calculated | Invested | Settled |
| Capitalized | Managed | Sold |
| Cast | Marketed | Totaled |
| Computed | Measured | Tracked |
| Conserved | Multiplied | Traded |
| Corrected | Netted | Transacted |
| Counted | Paid | Underwrote |
| Depreciated | Planned | Valued |
| Determined | Predicted | |

## Helping Skills

Accelerated
Accompanied
Adapted
Advanced
Advocated
Aided
Amplified
Answered
Arranged
Assessed
Assisted
Augmented
Availed
Boosted
Broadened
Championed
Clarified
Coached
Collaborated
Committed
Complied
Contributed
Cooperated
Counseled
Cultivated
Decreased
Demonstrated
Diagnosed
Dissected
Doubled
Eased
Educated
Effected
Encouraged
Endorsed

Energized
Enlarged
Ensured
Exceeded
Expanded
Expedited
Extended
Facilitated
Familiarized
Finalized
Fixed
Fostered
Fulfilled
Functioned
Furthered
Gave
Granted
Guided
Halted
Heightened
Helped
Honed
Insured
Intervened
Leveraged
Lifted
Lightened
Maximized
Minimized
Motivated
Offered
Offset
Played
Preserved
Prevented

Prompted
Propelled
Protected
Provided
Raised
Recommended
Reconciled
Recovered
Referred
Regained
Rehabilitated
Remedied
Represented
Resolved
Reversed
Salvaged
Satisfied
Served
Serviced
Shortened
Simplified
Stabilized
Substantiated
Supplied
Supported
Sustained
Targeted
Tightened
Treated
Tripled
Troubleshot
Vitalized
Volunteered
Weighed
Widened

## Interpersonal Skills

Addressed
Advertised
Aired
Approached
Arbitrated
Arranged
Articulated
Asked
Attracted
Authored
Bargained
Briefed
Called
Canvassed
Captured
Circulated
Clarified
Coauthored
Collaborated
Communicated
Composed
Condensed
Conferred
Consulted
Contacted
Conveyed
Convinced
Corresponded
Debated
Defined
Delivered
Described
Developed
Differed
Directed
Disclosed
Discussed
Drafted
Edited
Elicited

Enlisted
Exhibited
Explained
Expressed
Fielded
Formulated
Furnished
Greeted
Illuminated
Incorporated
Influenced
Inquired
Interacted
Interpreted
Interviewed
Invited
Involved
Joined
Judged
Justified
Lectured
Listened
Litigated
Lobbied
Marketed
Mediated
Met
Met with
Moderated
Motivated
Narrated
Negotiated
Noticed
Observed
Outlined
Participated
Persuaded
Polled
Presented
Profiled

Promoted
Proofread
Proposed
Publicized
Questioned
Reacted
Read
Reconciled
Recruited
Referred
Reinforced
Related
Renegotiated
Reported
Requested
Resolved
Responded
Shared
Showed
Signed
Solicited
Specified
Spoke
Spread
Stressed
Suggested
Summarized
Synthesized
Testified
Translated
Traveled
Verbalized
Viewed
Visited
Welcomed
Witnessed
Won
Wrote

## Management/Leadership Skills

Adhered
Administered
Admitted
Analyzed
Appointed
Approved
Assigned
Assumed
    responsibility
Attained
Authorized
Awarded
Blazed
Chaired
Closed
Commissioned
Considered
Consolidated
Continued
Contracted
Controlled
Converted
Coordinated
Decided
Delegated
Designated
Developed
Directed
Dispatched
Dispensed
Diversified
Elected
Eliminated
Emphasized
Enacted
Enforced

Enhanced
Established
Evaluated
Executed
Gained
Generated
Governed
Handled
Headed
Hired
Hosted
Implemented
Improved
Incorporated
Increased
Initiated
Inspected
Instituted
Issued
Kept
Launched
Led
Liquidated
Managed
Merged
Mobilized
Motivated
Navigated
Orchestrated
Organized
Oriented
Originated
Outsourced
Overcame
Overhauled
Oversaw

Passed
Penalized
Permitted
Piloted
Pioneered
Planned
Prescribed
Presided
Prioritized
Produced
Pursued
Ran
Rated
Received
Recommended
Reinstated
Rejected
Reorganized
Replaced
Restored
Reviewed
Rewarded
Safeguarded
Scheduled
Secured
Selected
Spearheaded
Staffed
Steered
Streamlined
Strengthened
Supervised
Surpassed
Terminated
Took
Undertook

## *Organizational Skills*

| | | |
|---|---|---|
| Approved | Interpreted | Reshaped |
| Arranged | Interviewed | Responded |
| Catalogued | Inventoried | Restructured |
| Categorized | Investigated | Retained |
| Centralized | Localized | Retrieved |
| Channeled | Logged | Revamped |
| Charted | Maintained | Reviewed |
| Checked | Mapped | Routed |
| Classified | Monitored | Scheduled |
| Cleared | Moved | Screened |
| Coded | Normalized | Segmented |
| Collected | Obtained | Separated |
| Compiled | Operated | Shrank |
| Corrected | Ordered | Sorted |
| Corresponded | Organized | Specified |
| Cut | Patterned | Standardized |
| Decentralized | Phased | Structured |
| Diagrammed | Pinpointed | Submitted |
| Dispatched | Placed | Supplied |
| Distributed | Prepared | Synchronized |
| Diverted | Processed | Systematized |
| Documented | Provided | Tabulated |
| Executed | Purchased | Traced |
| Filed | Put | Transferred |
| Formalized | Ranked | Transformed |
| Generated | Realigned | Transitioned |
| Grouped | Recorded | Transported |
| Identified | Recycled | Unified |
| Implemented | Refined | United |
| Incorporated | Registered | Updated |
| Indexed | Repositioned | Validated |
| Inspected | Reserved | Verified |

## Research Skills

| | | |
|---|---|---|
| Analyzed | Explored | Proved |
| Ascertained | Exposed | Reasoned |
| Carried out | Extracted | Recognized |
| Clarified | Formulated | Researched |
| Collected | Found | Revealed |
| Compared | Gathered | Reviewed |
| Concluded | Hypothesized | Searched |
| Conducted | Identified | Solved |
| Critiqued | Inspected | Speculated |
| Detected | Interviewed | Summarized |
| Determined | Invented | Surveyed |
| Diagnosed | Investigated | Systematized |
| Discovered | Located | Tested |
| Evaluated | Measured | Uncovered |
| Examined | Organized | |
| Experimented | Probed | |

## Teaching Skills

| | | |
|---|---|---|
| Adapted | Evaluated | Led |
| Advised | Explained | Mentored |
| Assessed | Facilitated | Motivated |
| Clarified | Focused | Persuaded |
| Coached | Graded | Presented |
| Communicated | Graduated | Reviewed |
| Conducted | Guided | Simulated |
| Coordinated | Individualized | Stimulated |
| Critiqued | Informed | Substituted |
| Developed | Initiated | Taught |
| Enabled | Inspired | Tested |
| Encouraged | Instilled | Trained |
| Engaged | Instructed | Transmitted |
| Enriched | Learned | Tutored |

### *Technical Skills*

| | | |
|---|---|---|
| Adapted | Fit out/up | Remodeled |
| Applied | Fortified | Repaired |
| Assembled | Installed | Replaced |
| Automated | Interfaced | Restored |
| Built | Maintained | Sent |
| Calculated | Manipulated | Set up |
| Computed | Manufactured | Sketched |
| Conserved | Merchandised | Solved |
| Constructed | Modernized | Specialized |
| Converted | Operated | Standardized |
| Debugged | Optimized | Studied |
| Designed | Overhauled | Trained |
| Determined | Printed | Transcribed |
| Developed | Programmed | Typed |
| Devised | Rectified | Upgraded |
| Engineered | Redesigned | Used |
| Fabricated | Regulated | Utilized |

# Cover Letters

Never submit your resume to a potential employer without a personalized cover letter. Include a cover letter if you are

- sending a resume in response to a classified ad, job posting, or job opening announcement.
- following up on a potential job lead given to you by an acquaintance.
- sending an unsolicited resume to a company.
- submitting your resume electronically, via a company's website.
- requesting that a contact review your resume.

We recommend that you keep your cover letter brief—introduce yourself and briefly explain your relevant career goals, experience, and abilities. Try to convince the reader that you're the perfect candidate for the position. Always invite the reader to contact you for an interview so they can get to learn more about you. Be sure to include information that shows you paid careful attention to the specific details and job requirements in the posting or ad. In your opening paragraph, make reference to the exact job title as it is advertised and where you found the advertisement.

When printing your cover letter, use a good printer and quality paper in a standard color—white, gray, or ivory. Always bring extra copies of your cover letter when going on an interview.

## Cover Letter Writing Tips

- Target your letter directly to the decision-making person by name whenever possible, to avoid having it sit in a general mailbox.
- Grab an employer's attention by pointing out how you can make a difference in ways that no other candidate can.
- Highlight your key accomplishments and what you could bring to the company—without restating your entire resume.
- Your cover letter should be sharp, focused, and free of errors.
- End your letter by including next steps, such as scheduling an interview, and be sure to include your contact information.

## What to Say

When potential employers read your letter, they'll be looking for answers to certain questions. Make sure your letter answers the following questions:

- Are you knowledgeable about the industry and the company?
- Can you communicate well on paper?

- Do you possess the skills, education, and work experience necessary to meet the job's qualifications?
- Do you have what it takes to succeed at the company?
- What sets you apart from other applicants?
- If you mention that you'll be making a follow-up phone call, be sure to give a potential employer at least three to five business days to read your cover letter and resume.

Whenever possible, your cover letter should be addressed to a specific individual. If you don't know the name of the person to whom you are sending the cover letter, it may be worth your while to do some sleuthing to find out. Often, this is as simple as searching online or calling the company and requesting the name and title of the person responsible for hiring. While you are on the line, confirm the correct spelling of the recipient's name. Repeat the information back to the person to whom you are speaking, so that you know you are correct. Spelling someone's name incorrectly is unprofessional and could land your resume in the trash bin even if you are a qualified candidate.

If you're sure the recipient of your letter is a woman, use "Dear Ms. (insert last name):" as your salutation. "Miss" is rarely used in business correspondence, and "Mrs." should only be used to address someone who is married. Some names are shared by both men and women. Don't make gender assumptions—they could easily be wrong. Call the company and ask for clarification if needed.

If a title of distinction, such as Doctor (Dr.), Reverend, or Professor, is listed in the ad, use it in your salutation. Write "Dear Dr. (insert last name):" or "Dear Reverend (insert last name):". The person who wrote the ad took the time to consider titles, so you should pay careful attention to using them correctly and appropriately.

When writing a salutation, avoid using "To Whom It May Concern" whenever possible. It's impersonal and may show that you didn't take the time to determine whom the letter should be sent to. Also avoid using the traditional salutation "Dear Sir or Madam." It's no longer considered proper for use in professional correspondence.

### What Not to Say

Topics to avoid in your cover letter include

- your age, race, religion, and health, including any physical or mental disabilities
- your hobbies
- your Social Security number
- references to your physical appearance

Do not mention compensation unless an employer asks for salary requirements. In these cases, provide a range, not a specific dollar amount.

Some job listings explicitly state "No calls or emails" or "Only qualified candidates will be contacted." If you're asked not to follow up, then don't mention that you will in your cover letter. Saying you'll follow up will not make you appear more eager for the job; it will only show that you're unable to follow simple instructions.

### Proofreading

Always proofread your cover letter for errors. Make sure that key dates and contact information are correct. If possible, have someone you trust proofread your cover letter as well. Remember, this is your opportunity to make a great first impression!

### Sample Letter 1

Veronica's cover letter shows that she has the background and experience needed to be a successful activities director. Notice how she clearly highlights her years of relevant work experience and accomplishments as an activities coordinator, and she even turns her volunteer experience into an asset. She mentions why working for this company in particular is so attractive to her and closes strongly with an interview request.

**Ms. Veronica Martinez**
1010 Winwood Way
San Diego, CA 90000
555-555-1234
vmartinez@mail.com

May 15, 2015
Kara Rush
Human Resources Director
Memory Lane Assisted Living Centers of California
2999 Sawchuk Lane
San Diego, CA 90000

Dear Ms. Rush:

I am writing in response to your advertisement for an activities director in the May 14, 2015 edition of the *Daily Times*. In my enclosed resume, you will find that I have the skills and work experience necessary to fill this position.

I have more than four years of experience working for the Tiny Tykes Day Care Center as an activities coordinator. During this time, I have created new activities programs, including a series of month-long programs designed to enhance cognitive and physical development.

I have supplemented my employment experience with considerable volunteer work at the Golden Sunset Nursing Home. This experience has enabled me to combine my skills in activities development with my interest in caring for the aged.

Based on your company's thirteen-year track record as a leading assisted-living center in California, I would be honored to be part of your activities department. My combination of proven success and innovation at Tiny Tykes Day Care Center, along with my experience motivating seniors and staff at the Golden Sunset Nursing Home, would be beneficial to Memory Lane as you refine your activities programs throughout the state.

Thank you for considering me for the activities director position at Memory Lane Assisted Living Centers of California. I look forward to speaking with you in greater detail about this job opportunity. Please contact me by phone or email to schedule an interview.

Sincerely,

Veronica Martinez

### *Sample Letter 2*

Pamela takes an interesting approach in her cover letter. She opens with a short anecdote about her childhood, which hopefully draws in her target audience. Personal angles like this may be risky to take in a more formal letter-writing context, but because she is a college student just getting started, it may show her readers that she has personality that can translate into her work. She works hard to convince readers that her experience, energy, and enthusiasm would make her an outstanding intern and then ties in her qualifications. Pamela is well on her way to landing her dream internship!

**Pamela Greene**
15 Avenue G, Apartment B • Washington, DC 55555 • 202-555-5555
pamela.greene@yourdomain.com • http://www.linkedin.com/in/
pamelagreene

May 20, 2015

Xavier Monopoly
1 Washington Street, Suite 505
Washington, DC 55555

Dear Mr. Monopoly:
With five children, my parents did not have much time for extras. You could say that recycling was not high on their list of things to investigate. I saw a movie at school when I was in second grade about how we can each help save the planet by doing our part to reduce waste. Starting then, I knew what I wanted to do when I grew up. I've been the environmentally conscious member of my family ever since and have made sure my family has been recycling. I would be thrilled to bring my energy, skills, and enthusiasm to serve as a Green Seal Summer Intern, as advertised on GreenJobsGo.com.

My major at the University of Virginia is Environmental Sciences. I have gained a significant foundation in the "hows and whys" regarding our planet's benefit if everyone changes their habits. I welcome the opportunity to put that knowledge to work to contribute to your mission, "Save the planet, one person at a time." I hope you agree that my skills and experiences qualify me to work with you.

One phrase that comes up over and over again on my evaluations and endorsements is "team player." I pride myself on being able to work with all types of groups to get the job done. Recently, I headed a team of five other students to organize "Recycle Day" in our residence hall. I made sure we each had a job and followed through. The result was a successful day that changed many minds about the value of each individual's contribution to the environment.

As leader of UVA's Green Group, I've had many opportunities to speak about our initiatives to organizations on campus and to local school children. It's no small feat to be able to capture the imaginations of skeptical college kids and attention-challenged first graders, but my programs have received rave reviews! I help support our mission using my writing skills and initiated a newsletter that is distributed across campus. It has been so successful and well received that we have been able to sell enough ads to more than support our club's expenditures.

Please review my attached resume and visit my LinkedIn page to read recommendations and other information that show I am a perfect match for the Green Seal Internship. I look forward to the opportunity to speak with you more about the position and my experiences.

Sincerely,

Pamela Greene

## *Sample Letter 3*

Vincent is looking for helpful information about a possible culinary career with his letter. Requesting a job shadow can be a smart move—it's a good way to learn more about an industry and can also open up new networking opportunities.

---

**Vincent Orlando**
123 Orchard Street, San Diego, CA 55555, 555-555-5555
vince.orlando@yourdomain.com

May 15, 2015

Rueben Cesaria
Le Singe Verte
San Diego, CA 12345

Dear Mr. Cesaria:

I am currently a senior at St. Augustine High School and seriously considering a career as a chef in the fine dining market. I have been accepted to the French Culinary Institute for the Fall semester and would greatly appreciate the experience of shadowing a world-renowned chef at a popular, high-end restaurant such as Le Singe Verte.

I realize that you are quite busy running a bustling kitchen, but I would consider it an honor to witness your unquestionable mastery as a chef. While I am certainly familiar with the inner workings of a busy kitchen, having worked as a busboy, waiter, prep cook, and ultimately head cook at my family's restaurant from the age of 10, I would greatly appreciate the opportunity to view a three-star Michelin-rated team at work.

Thank you very much for considering my request. I will be available at your convenience to set up an appointment for this shadowing experience, and I look forward to hearing from you soon.

Thank you, once again, for your time and attention.

Sincerely,

Vincent Orlando

---

# Section 2: Writing Basics

**P**eople sometimes assume that writing in the workplace must be stiff and formal, even stuffy. While highly formal writing was typical in the past, many businesses, from corporate enterprises to the nonprofit sector, now embrace a more conversational style—as long as it remains professional. The most important considerations for tone are sounding confident, courteous, and sincere.

Expressing yourself clearly is crucial in business communications. Imagine a manager making a decision about what product to offer based on miscalculated data or an employee getting the wrong message about what days can be taken off from work. If you state your thoughts in a way that can be misinterpreted, your reader may end up drawing the wrong conclusions—and acting on them might have disastrous consequences.

In this this section on fundamental skills, you will learn how to analyze your audience and write clearly and concisely—and still manage to be yourself in your writing.

# 2 Know Your Audience

There is no way around it: the only way to write successfully in the workplace is to understand your audience. It is a simple theory that is put into practice in the one million subtleties of our everyday lives. If you are in a restaurant where the server takes great care to get your individual order right, makes all the changes you requested, and even makes you feel like he is tending to you alone, you won't notice the other tables he's waiting on. You will probably even give him a great tip. You both come away happy. Or, if a doctor really listens to you, carefully collects all your information, and treats you with respect, you will not only remain loyal to that doctor, but you may even refer friends to him or her. These are both examples of successful relationships that exist because someone took the time to understand his or her audience.

As a writer, you want to get your point across first and foremost, so make it easy for the reader. If you are able to put yourself in your reader's shoes, your correspondence will be well received. Your reader will feel comfortable building a relationship with you, and you will have earned that reader's trust and, hopefully, his or her business. This applies to clients, colleagues, supervisors, and subordinates—everyone. Listen, learn, and succeed.

## Who Is Your Audience?

Figuring out who will be reading your work is every bit as important as determining what you will say in your writing. For example, consider the following writing projects:

- 500 words on trends in your industry.
- 250 words on why you deserve a raise.
- 150-word thank you note to a client.
- a 15-word email to a colleague.
- a journal entry (as long as you like) on your five year career plan.

Who will be your audience (your reader or readers) for each of these texts? If you are applying for a grant, you will want to address yourself to the deciding committee and try to provide reasons for choosing you that will appeal to them. On the other hand, if you're writing to a personal friend, you can refer to private jokes and assume that your friend is already familiar with you and your sense of humor.

## Audience Analysis Questions

Audience analysis deserves serious attention, regardless of who your audience is. And it entails more than just learning a few bland statistics, such as your reader's company and position. Following are important questions to consider:

- What is the reader's age, sex, present job, educational level, and past experience?
- What is the reader's primary spoken language?

- How does the reader prefer to be addressed?
- What form of business communication does the reader use most? An executive from a leading computer company says she does not look at anything but electronic correspondence—emailing her would be your best bet.
- What type of clientele does the reader serve?
- What is the reader's demeanor—conservative or moderate?
- At what level of authority is the reader? Can he or she act on your letter?
- What matters most to the reader in a written document? Does he prefer brevity to details? Does he have disdain for unwarranted attachments? Or, does he prefer to have everything possible sent to him?
- Does the reader have a sense of humor? Will he or she be able to understand your sense of humor?
- What type of business language is the reader accustomed to? Technical lingo, medical lingo, legalese, and so on?

These are examples of questions that will help you understand your audience. As you build your professional relationships, you will be able to dig into even finer details about your reader that will personalize and enhance your communication.

## Communication Style and Tone

It is critical to use a communication style and tone that fits your audience. You wouldn't write the same thing to your mother as you would to a prospective client. But you do need to always remember the human element in your business writing. In today's technical age, it is more important than ever to personalize your messages. So, once you have analyzed your reader, try to strike the balance between professional and too cozy. It's best to err on the side of warmth—don't be stuffy and cold.

Use simple, direct communication that is geared straight to the reader. No one will ever complain that your letters are too easy to read or that he or she understood them too well.

An executive for a high-tech company says this about getting in touch with your audience:

*As a company, we make a conscious effort to cut back on the technical jargon when writing or speaking to our clients. Using jargon only makes your clients feel inferior and self-conscious. People want to be around those who make them feel good. Therefore, if we want to build lasting client relationships, we need to understand our audience and communicate at their level.*

An executive vice president of a leading medical malpractice insurance company offers an excellent illustration of how important it is to understand your audience, especially when they are also your colleagues.

*We have a beautiful office building in the wine country of Northern California. We also had a serious peacock problem on the grounds outside of our beautiful building. What began as two lonely peacocks turned into a flock of cousins, uncles, aunts, and young peacock offspring.*

*The employees took to the budding peacock family, and began feeding them and treating them as pets. Before long, we had peacocks flying to our outdoor lunch tables, even disrupting some lunch meetings. Have you ever seen a peacock fly? We knew we had to do something.*

*So I wrote a company-wide letter, asking all employees to please refrain from feeding the peacocks, as they were not our pets. I realized halfway through my letter that, in a company of more than 300 employees, there were some who were sensitive to animal rights issues. So, I had to gear my letter to the most sensitive person. If I was too blunt or careless in my tone, it could have affected employee morale and caused bigger issues than flying peacocks. In the end, a letter that I thought would be simple to write—easy issue, not a million-dollar deal—turned out to be a good lesson in understanding my whole audience.*

# Analyzing Audience Characteristics

It is just as important to understand the thinking style of your reader as it is to understand your own. Many different theories have been studied over the years about individual personalities and how people think. And, in an age where understanding the people behind the machines is becoming increasingly important, we need to pay special attention to this subject. Carl Jung theorized that there are four basic styles of communication:

1. *Sensor/Action Style*
   These people are action-oriented and very hands-on. They are driven, determined, tough, competitive, confident, and assertive. They can also be domineering, arrogant, and impersonal. Typical careers for this person include doctor, athlete, executive, and pilot.

2. *Thinker/Process Style*
   These people are information-processors. They organize and strategize, as well as gather information. They are analytical, logical, critical, methodical, organized, and persistent. They can also be insensitive and judgmental or inflexible. Typical careers for this person include lawyer, engineer, scientist, and financier.

3. *Feeler/People Style*
   These people are socially geared, communicative, team-oriented, warm, friendly, and persuasive. They can also be subjective, overly sensitive, and overly cautious. Typical careers for this person include teacher, psychologist, and sales associate.

4. *Intuitors/Idea Style*

These people are creative, theory-oriented, and driven by ideas. They are reflective, serene, "dreamers," adventurous, and flexible. They can also be undisciplined with time, unrealistic, and manipulative. Typical careers for this person include artist, professor, researcher, and writer.

It is important to note that these are simply theories that Carl Jung used to try to categorize certain personality traits that he observed. You or your reader could be a combination of any of these descriptions—or, you could seemingly not fit any particular category.

So, pay close attention to your reader, and be careful not to make personality assumptions based solely on occupation when you're cultivating the tone of your prose.

Once you understand what type of communication style your reader uses, then you can decide what kind of tone and correspondence is appropriate to the situation. Here are some examples of how tone can shift, depending on the audience.

### Informal Note

*Hey, Jacob, did you hear Perry's on board? We think his business development experience at R & G Corrugation will really help us acquire new business partners—especially in manufacturing. He's already presented some awesome ideas.*

### Company Newsletter

*Please join us in welcoming Perry Taft to Fitch's business development team. Perry's experience at R & G Corrugation, Inc., contacts in the manufacturing business, and infectious enthusiasm were central reasons for bringing him on board. Welcome, Perry! We know you will be a valued new asset at Fitch Corporation.*

### Press Release

*Fitch Corporation, the nation's leader in corrugation manufacturing, announced today the hiring of Perry Taft to the position of Vice President of Business Development. Taft brings more than 15 years of business development experience from R & G Corrugation, Inc.*

With the pace of communication in today's world, you need to write so that people can understand you. You need to get into the mind of your reader and really tap into what will make a difference and what will elicit a positive response. This requires listening, learning, and thinking about what you want to say, and to whom you are saying it, *before* you write. If you put yourself in your reader's shoes, you will both enjoy strong communication and a better business relationship.

So, you need to get personal. Learn what makes each person tick. Who are they? Where are they coming from? What is most important to them? When you have gathered what you need to know about your reader, use a communication style that is audience appropriate. Then decide what type of correspondence fits the situation—personal note, formal letter, press release. Once you are clear about to *whom* you are writing, it is time to be clear about *what* you are writing.

## Practice: Identifying Audience, Point of View, and Style

Imagine you are planning what to write texts for three different projects. In the following chart, fill in brief descriptions of an appropriate audience, point of view, and style for each project. An example of a response is provided.

| PROJECT | AUDIENCE | POINT OF VIEW | STYLE OR TONE |
|---|---|---|---|
| A movie review | I'm going to put my review on my blog, so my audience is my readers and (I hope) new friends. | I am going to say right at the top of my review that I hated the movie, and then readers will know my point of view. | I'm going to try to be funny and casual since I'm writing for other movie fans. |
| 1. my performance self-evaluation | | | |
| 2. A new project proposal | | | |
| 3. A meeting summary memo | | | |

There are no right or wrong answers here. Don't rush: take your time and plan carefully. You may well be able to use the planning work you do here in subsequent chapters.

# 3 Writing With Clarity

**W**illiam Strunk said it vividly: "Make every word tell." His classic book, *The Elements of Style*, is only 85 pages long, and it remains one of the best books ever written on the subject of writing. He understood that he would lose his audience after the first page if he didn't write clearly and concisely. As a professor, he repeated his mantra to classrooms packed with riveted students: "Omit needless words!" He apparently said it with such force and determination that many of them never forgot. And neither should you.

Many of the best-written works of all time are clear and concise. Take our Constitution's Bill of Rights, for example. It is only one page long; though the print is very small, it said enough in that single page to run one of the most powerful countries on Earth for more than 200 years. If our forefathers can lay the foundation for an entire country on one large sheet of paper, then we can certainly be clear and concise with our business correspondence and letters.

# Techniques for Clear Writing

Is there one technique that you can use in all of your business correspondence? Yes! Be consistent with your clarity and simplicity. Pretend that you are the captain of a sinking ship and you have only a few sentences to get your message out to your entire crew. This means that you have to write in a way that is understandable to everyone, from the ship's cook to the navigator.

An executive in the insurance industry said this about his business communication:

> *In more than 40 years of business, I always used the same technique: plain, simple, understandable, and to the point. You can't go wrong that way—it leaves no room for confusion or misinterpretation.*

The COO for a technical company took a business writing class in which the instructor had a mathematical formula for grading the writing. It was simple—those who wrote the shortest sentences and used the simplest words got the highest scores. The class learned that clarifying and simplifying their prose led to drastically increased understanding of the message content.

They got the point of the message. No one became bogged down trying to decipher difficult words or having to wade through murky sentences. So, try scoring yourself—write a sample letter and have a friend or associate read it. Ask him or her to score each sentence by giving 10 points for every concise statement and subtracting 10 points for every confusing statement. If your first score is on the low side, never fear! That only means you have room for growth and a new opportunity to make yourself an even better writer than you thought you could be.

## Be Clear

There was an orator named Demosthenes who lived in Athens, Greece, in 300 B.C. He was highly praised by everyone for being a brilliant communicator because he used lofty words that made him sound intelligent. His style was animated and captivating. The people got so caught up in listening to him that they never knew what he was actually saying. One day he proclaimed another orator to be better than he. He said simply that, when the other man spoke, he spoke to the level of the crowd, and they heard his *message*. They left his speeches knowing what he had said. Thousands of years later, the same theory applies—be clear above all. Your most important objective is to get your message heard.

An executive vice president with more than 17,000 employees under his direction says this about clarity:

*Write like you would talk to a friend. This may be [risky], but it is clearer and establishes your style. For example, "Charley, it is time we sat down face-to-face and talked this deal over," instead of, "At your earliest convenience, would you please extend your permission to arrange a mutually agreeable time to convene a business meeting to discuss . . . blah, blah, blah."*

The funny thing is that "blah, blah, blah" is probably exactly what the reader would be thinking if they received the latter note. So, think like an executive vice president—a leader—and get to the point with your writing.

If you think and write like a leader, you will eventually *become* a leader. Leaders have a clear direction. They have a clear goal. And they cut a path straight to that goal. This means that it is absolutely critical to pay attention throughout your writing process. If you have total clarity about what you want—and don't be afraid to get specific—then make the decision to go after it, keep focused, and sharpen your writing until it glistens like a blade in sunlight.

# Wordiness

Excess words in communication waste space and time. Not only that, but they may also distort the message or make it difficult for the reader to understand. Get in the habit of streamlining your writing, making the sentences as concise as possible. If you use five words where three would do, delete the extra words or structure your sentences to avoid them.

See if you can rewrite the sentences in the first column to make them less wordy. Check yourself against the version in the second column.

| WORDY | REVISED |
| --- | --- |
| It was a three-hour period after the accident when the rescue squad that we knew was going to help us arrived. [21 words] | The rescue squad arrived three hours after the accident. [9 words] |
| It was decided that the church would organize a committee for the purpose of conducting a search for a new pastor. [21 words] | The church organized a committee to search for a new pastor. [11 words] |

The additional words in the first column add no information. All they do is take up space.

## Redundancy

A writing trap that takes up space is *redundancy*, repeating words that express the same idea or in which the meanings overlap. If you stop to think about phrases like the following—and many others—you'll see that the extra words are not only unnecessary but often just plain silly.

> enclosed *with this letter*
> remit *payment*
> *absolutely* necessary

weather *outside*
postpone *until later*
refer *back*
*past* history
ask *the question*
continue *on*
proceed *ahead*
repeated *over again*
gather *together*
*compulsory* requirement
*temporarily* suspended
*necessary* requirements
plain *and simple*

*Enclosed* means it's in the letter, doesn't it? *Remit* means *pay.* And how can something be more *necessary* than *necessary?* The weather *outside* as opposed to the weather *inside? Past* history as opposed to . . . ? You see the point. Keep it simple. (Not *plain and simple.*)

## Buzzwords and Modifiers

Buzzwords—such as *aspect, element, factor, scope, situation, type, kind, forms,* and so on—sound important but add no meaning to a sentence. They often signal a writer who has little or nothing to say yet wishes to sound important. Likewise, modifiers such as *absolutely, definitely, really, very, important, significant, current, major,* and *quite* may add length to a sentence, but they seldom add meaning.

**Wordy:**

The *nature of the* scheduling system is a *very important matter* that can *definitely* have a *really significant* impact on the morale *aspect* of an employee's attitude. *Aspects of* our current scheduling policy make it *absolutely necessary* that we undergo a *significant* change.

**Revised:**

The scheduling system can affect employee morale. Our policy needs to be changed.

The following table lists a host of phrases that can be reduced to one or two words.

| WORDY | CONCISE | WORDY | CONCISE |
|---|---|---|---|
| puzzling in nature | puzzling | at this point in time | now; today |
| of a peculiar kind | peculiar | at that point in time | then |
| regardless of the fact that | although | in order to | to |
| due to the fact that | because | by means of | by |
| of an indefinite nature | indefinite | exhibits a tendency to | tends to |
| concerning the matter of | about | in connection with | with |
| in the event that | if | in relation to | with |

# Practice 1: Eliminating Redundancy

Rewrite the following sentences to make them less wordy.

1. It gives us great pleasure to take this opportunity to announce the opening of the newly built playground at the Municipal Park in Succasunna.

2. It is certainly a true statement that bears repeating over and over again that technological advancements such as

computers can assist employees in performing in a very efficient manner, and that these self-same computers may in fact result in considerable savings over a period of time.

**3.** I arrived at a decision to allow the supervisor of my department to achieve a higher golf score in order to enhance my opportunities for advancement in the event that such opportunities became available.

## Passive Voice

Some wordiness is caused by using passive voice when you could use active voice. The **active voice** directly connects the action with the person who is performing that action. The **passive voice** renders the *doer* of the action less obvious, if that person is ever identified at all. The active voice is concise and energetic, and it is the preferred writing style.

**Active Voice:** We recommend you file a claim.
**Passive Voice:** It is recommended that you file a claim.

**Active Voice:** Let's meet soon.
**Passive Voice:** A meeting should be held as soon as possible.

Even though the active voice is more straightforward, there are times when the passive voice is necessary:

**1.** When you don't know who the subject is:
   *Our proposal was submitted late because critical details were still missing.*
**2.** When you want to emphasize the receiver:
   *Hannah was accepted at Harvard Medical School.*

3. When you want to put some variation into your text or smooth thought transition:

> *This year's Holiday Party will be held at Snoqualmie Falls ski lodge. It should be a warm and festive celebration—see you there!*

# Practice 2: Eliminating Passive Voice

Revise the sentences to eliminate passive voice.

1. It has been decided that your application for grant money is not in accordance with the constraints outlined by the committee in the application guidelines.

2. The letter of resignation was accepted by the Board of Directors.

### Intellectual-ese

Some sentences suffer not only from passive-voice wordiness, but also from the writer's attempt to sound intellectual—making the message more difficult than necessary. Writers make this error in many ways. One way is to turn adjectives and verbs into nouns. This transformation usually means extra words are added to the sentence.

| WORDY | REVISED |
| --- | --- |
| Water pollution [noun] is not as serious in the northern parts of Canada. | Water is not as polluted [adjective] in northern Canada. |
| Customer demand [noun] is reducing in the area of sales services. | Customers demand [verb] fewer sales services. |

Sometimes when writers add words without adding meaning, the result is a pretentious tone. What follows is an actual memo issued by a bureaucrat during World War II. When it was sent to President Franklin Roosevelt for his approval, he edited it before sending it on.

**Original memo:**
In the unlikely event of an attack by an invader of a foreign nature, such preparations shall be made as will completely obscure all Federal buildings and non-Federal buildings occupied by the Federal government during an air raid for any period of time from visibility by reason of internal or external illumination.

**Roosevelt's revised memo:**
If there is an air raid, put something across the windows and turn off the lights outside in buildings where we have to keep the work going.

Here's another example of pretentious writing, along with a clearer, revised version.

**Original memo:**
As per the most recent directive issued from this office, it is incumbent upon all employees and they are henceforth instructed to reduce in amount the paper used in the accomplishment of their daily tasks due to the marked increase in the cost of such supplies.

**Revised:**
Since paper costs have increased, employees must use less paper.

The following table illustrates sentences that have been rewritten more concisely.

| WORD ECONOMY | |
| --- | --- |
| **STRETCHED SENTENCE** | **CONCISE SENTENCE** |
| Cassandra seems to be content. | Cassandra seems content. |
| We must know what it is that we are doing. | We must know what we're doing. |
| This is the book of which I have been speaking. | I spoke about this book. |
| It is with pleasure that I announce the winner. | I am pleased to announce the winner. |
| The reason we were late was because of traffic. | We were late because of traffic. |
| These plans will be considered on an individual basis. | These plans will be considered individually. |
| The caterer, who was distressed, left the party. | The distressed caterer left the party. |
| There are new shipments arriving daily. | New shipments arrive daily. |
| Due to the fact that we were late, we missed the door prizes. | We came late and missed the door prizes. |
| The consideration given in the latest promotion is an example of how I was treated unfairly. | I was not fairly considered for the latest promotion. |

# Precise Language

Make your writing as precise as possible. In doing so, you communicate more meaning. Choose exact verbs, modifiers, and nouns to help you transmit an exact meaning, such as in the following examples.

| IMPRECISE VERSUS PRECISE | |
|---|---|
| **VERBS** | |
| Emilia participated in the protest. | Emilia organized the march on the capital. |
| Hannah won't deal with sales meetings. | Hannah won't attend sales meetings. |
| Dick can relate to Jane. | Dick understands Jane's feelings. |
| **MODIFIERS** | |
| These bad instructions confused me. | These disorganized, vague instructions left me with no idea how to repair the leak. |
| *Wall-E* is a good movie with fun for all. | *Wall-E* is a clever animated film with humor, adventure, and romance. |
| We had a nice time with you. | We enjoyed eating your food, drinking your wine, and swimming in your pool. |
| **NOUNS** | |
| I always have trouble with this computer. | I can never get this computer to save or print. |
| I like to have fun when I take a vacation. | I like to swim, fish, and eat out when I'm on vacation. |
| Let me grab some things from my office. | Let me grab my purse and books from my office. |

## Abstract versus Concrete

Abstract language refers to intangible ideas or to classes of people and objects rather than the people or things themselves. Abstractions are built on concrete ideas. Without a grasp of the concrete meanings, a reader can't be expected to understand an abstract idea. Journalists and law enforcement professionals are especially aware of the distinction between abstract and concrete as they write. They strive to present the facts clearly so the reader can draw conclusions. They avoid making the assumptions for the reader, hoping the facts will speak for themselves. Concrete language requires more time and thought to write, but it communicates a message more effectively. Additional words are an advantage if they add meaning or increase precision.

| ABSTRACT ASSUMPTION | CONCRETE DETAILS |
| --- | --- |
| Strader was amazing. | Strader scored 28 points, grabbed 12 rebounds, and blocked five shots. |
| The couple was in love. | The couple held hands, hugged, and ignored everything around them. |
| Billie is reliable and responsible. | Billie always arrives on time, completes her rotations, and helps others if she can. |

## Clichés

Authors use **clichés** when they don't have the time or ability to come up with more precise or meaningful language. Although clichés are a sort of communication shorthand, they rely on stereotypes for their meaning. A writer who uses clichés is relying on unoriginal, worn-out thinking patterns to carry a message. If the message is important, fresh language will make a stronger impression. Original language stimulates thought and heightens the reader's concentration. Moreover, a fresh image rewards an attentive reader.

There are countless clichés, but here are some of the most common ones found in business writing:

| | |
| --- | --- |
| add insult to injury | bottom line |
| back to the drawing board | business as usual |
| ballpark figure | clear the air |
| beat a dead horse | cream of the crop |
| behind the eight ball | dog-eat-dog |
| beside the point | dot the i's and cross the t's |

eleventh hour

few and far between

first and foremost

get a leg up on

grin and bear it

hand in glove

handwriting on the wall

heads will roll

hem and haw

heretofore

hit pay dirt

hit the nail on the head

if worse comes to worst

in a nutshell

knuckle under

last but not least

lesser of the two evils

letter perfect

low man on the totem pole

make ends meet

mark my words

meet your needs

movers and shakers

pack it in

pay the piper

point in time

rat race

roll with the punches

run it up the flagpole

spill the beans

state of the art

take the ball and run with it

too many irons in the fire

well and good

We tend to use clichés when we either don't know the information we're referring to or when we're unsure how to word something. Take a chance and be original! It shows you know your stuff—and, at the very least, you will be heard.

# Practice 3: Eliminating Cliché

Underline the instances of cliché in the following paragraph.

When it comes to fixing our nation's energy crisis, we need to think outside the box. We will need to roll up our sleeves and dig in, finding ways to reduce our current energy footprints while developing alternative forms of energy. Children are our future, and if we deplete this planet and leave them with no resources, we leave them up the creek without a paddle. Sustainability studies and research can show us the writing on the wall and highlight areas where we can be more "green" as a society. Information is our friend as we look to conserve, create, and maintain resources for a brighter tomorrow.

## *Jargon*

*Jargon* is the technical, wordy language used by those associated with a trade or profession. Often, it is full of passive voice, acronyms, technical terms, and abstract words. Writers use jargon to sound educated, sophisticated, or knowledgeable. Actually, jargon muddies and even distorts the message. Compare the following two paragraphs.

HCO, Inc. will develop a real-time interface between Lexor and Rocky Mountain Corp. This interface will be bidirectional, and assumes approximately ten business event transactions will be supported (based upon current design documentation). The interface will be implemented in an asynchronous fashion, to provide greater reliability and system scalability, using an event queuing/routing solution such as Microsoft BizSpeak.

HCO, Inc. will develop software that will allow Lexor and Rocky Mountain Corp. to communicate with each other instantly. Data can be transferred from Lexor to Rocky Mountain Corp., and vice versa. It will be transferred between the two systems in ten separate distinct events, which will be triggered by end-users in either system. When the data transfer process is triggered, the information will be placed in a queue for execution. The queuing of data transfer requests will allow for greater system reliability, and will also make it easier to grow the system, store more data, and/or add new features.Microsoft Biz-Speak will be used to support the queuing process.

The first version is filled with techno-jargon that would baffle any nontechnical person. The second is a much more understandable version—even if had to be a little *longer* to simplify.

When you write, strive for clear, plain language that communicates your message accurately. Clear communication leaves a better impression by far than pretentious, abstract, jargon-filled sentences.

## Practice 4: Clear and Concise Writing

Choose the option that expresses the idea most clearly and concisely.

1. **a.** Doubtless, the best choice we could make would reflect our association's founding principles.
   **b.** It is without a doubt that the most advantageous selection we could choose would be one that best reflects our association's principles that it has had since its origin.

2. **a.** The least expensive option in a situation such as this is inevitably also the most advantageous option.
   **b.** The cheapest way is the best way.

**3. a.** Too many youngsters prefer using their spare time with popular modern pastimes to improving their minds with more analytical options.

   **b.** Too many youths prefer using their spare time to play video games, instant message, and text message friends than to improve their minds with reading.

**4. a.** The marketing department found that customers prefer the vanilla scent.

   **b.** Consumer attitude studies conducted by our marketing department seem to indicate that a large majority of our customers had good things to say about the vanilla scent.

### ⇨ TIP

Listen to public officials as they deliver prepared speeches. Do they speak clearly and plainly, or are they trying to sound "official"? A truly competent, intelligent speaker or writer doesn't need a mask of pretentious, abstract, sophisticated-sounding language.

## Tone

**Tone** describes a writer's attitude toward the subject or the audience. The more reasonable and objective a message seems, the more likely it is to be considered seriously. Raging emotions seldom convince anyone to change an opinion, and they seldom convince anyone who is undecided. Persuasion requires clearly presented facts and logically presented arguments. A reader or listener will give the most credibility to a text that seems professional, fair, and objective.

### *Avoid Colloquialism*

Avoid chummy, informal language. **Colloquialisms** are informal words and phrases such as *a lot*, *in a bind*, *pulled it off*, and so on. These words and phrases are widely used in conversations between friends, but in written communication, they portray an attitude of chumminess or close friendship that may cause your message to be taken less seriously than you intended. A friendly, colloquial tone is fine in a personal letter; however, a more formal tone is better for business communications. Compare the following paragraphs. If you received these two memos from an employee, which would you take more seriously?

> I think the way we promote people around here stinks. People who aren't that good at their jobs get promoted just because they pal around with the right people. That puts across the idea that it doesn't matter how much time I put in at work or how good of a job I do; I won't get promoted unless I kiss up to the boss. I'm not that kind of guy.

> I think our promotion system is unfair. Average and below-average employees receive promotions simply because they befriend their superiors. This practice leaves the impression that commitment and quality of work are not considered. I choose not to socialize with my supervisors, and I feel as though I am not being promoted for that reason alone.

The writer of the first paragraph sounds as if he doesn't take his job all that seriously. And yet he probably does; he just hasn't managed to communicate his seriousness in writing because he has used language that is more appropriate in a conversation with his friends than a memo to his supervisor. The writer of the second paragraph, on the other hand, conveys his seriousness by using more formal language. He has done so without falling into the opposite trap, discussed earlier, of trying to sound *too* intelligent. He has used plain, but not colloquial, language.

The sentences in the following table illustrate the difference between colloquial and formal diction. By substituting the highlighted words, the sentence becomes more formal rather than colloquial.

| COLLOQUIAL | MORE FORMAL WORDS |
|---|---|
| I have **around** three hours to finish this task. | I have **approximately** three hours to finish this task. |
| The pasta was **real** good. | The pasta was **very** good. |
| We **got sick** from the food. | We **became ill** from the food. |
| It looks **like** we could win. | It looks **as if** we could win. |
| I'm **awful** tired. | I'm **very** (or **quite** or **extremely**) tired. |

# Practice 5: Avoiding Colloquialism

Underline the instances of colloquiliasm and improper tone.

Hey boss,

The presentation for tomorrow's meeting is ready. Fred and I were hanging out late last night, pulling together our research and our ideas so we could whip them into shape. After we were done, I emailed the dude over in the graphics department to finish the formatting. This morning, I eyeballed the information to make sure everything was included, and I think we're good to go. Lemme know if there's anything else you'd like me to do before tomorrow's meeting.

## *Avoid Anger*

Avoid accusatory, angry words that make demands. Consider the two paragraphs that follow. Which one is most likely to persuade the reader to take action?

> I just got this stupid credit card bill in the mail. None of these outrageous charges are mine. I can't believe some big corporation like yours can't find a way to keep its records straight or keep its customers from being cheated. If you can't do any better than that, why don't you just give it up? I reported my stolen credit card five days before any of these charges were made, and yet you idiots have charged me for these purchases. The fine print you guys are so fond of putting in all of your contracts says I am not (I'll say it again just to help you understand) not responsible for these charges. I want them removed immediately.

> The credit card bill I received on April 25 contains several charges that need to be removed. I reported my stolen credit card on April 20. When I called to make the report, the representative referred me to the original contract that states, "No charges in excess of $50.00 nor any made more than 24 hours after the card has been reported stolen shall be charged to the customer's account." Naturally, I was quite relieved. All of the charges on this account were made more than 24 hours after I reported the stolen card. Please remove the charges from my account. Thank you very much.

No matter how angry you might be, giving your reader the benefit of the doubt is not only polite but also more likely to get results. (This principle is especially important when you're writing a supervisor, employee, or client.) The first letter is the one you might write in the heat of the moment when you first get your credit card bill. In fact, writing that letter might help you get the anger out of your system. Tearing it up will make you feel even better. *Then* you can sit down and write the letter you're actually going to send—the second version.

Use **sarcasm** (bitter, derisive language) and **irony** (saying the opposite of what you actually mean) carefully in your writing. Like anger, sarcasm brings your credibility into question. Overusing sarcasm can make you seem childish or petty rather than reasonable and logical. For irony to be successful, the reader must immediately recognize it. Unless the reader fully understands, you risk confusing or distorting your message. A little well-placed irony or sarcasm may invigorate your writing, but it requires careful, skillful use.

## *Avoid Cuteness*

Avoid words that make your writing sound flippant, glib, or cute. Although the writing may be entertaining to the reader, it might not be taken seriously. The following paragraph protests a decision but fails to offer a single reason why the decision was wrong. It may get the attention of the reader, but it won't produce any results, except perhaps the dismissal of its author.

> I'm just a li'l ol' girl, but it's clear to me that this decision is dead wrong. I'm afraid that the people who made it have a serious intelligence problem. If they took their two IQ points and rubbed them together, they probably couldn't light gasoline on fire. If you were one of those people . . . Oh well, it's been nice working for you.

The conclusion implied in this writer's last sentence—that she won't work here much longer—is probably accurate.

## *Avoid Pompousness*

Avoid words that make your writing sound pompous or preachy. Few people respond positively to a condescending, patronizing tone. Compare the following two paragraphs, both written by employees seeking a promotion. Which employee would you promote if they were both vying for the same position and had nearly identical work records and qualifications?

If you examine my service and work record for the past two years, I believe you will find a dedicated, hardworking employee who is ideal for the floor manager position. I believe all employees should be on time for their jobs. You will see that my attendance record is impeccable, no absences and no tardies. You can see from my monthly evaluations that I was a high-quality employee when I was hired and that I have consistently maintained my high standards. I strive to be the kind of employee all managers wish to hire, and I believe my record shows this. I am also extremely responsible. Again, my record will reflect that my supervisors have confidence in me and assign additional responsibility readily to me because I am someone who can handle it. I am a man of my word, and I believe that responsibility is something to be treasured, not shirked. As you compare me with other employees, I feel confident that you will find I am the most competent person available.

Thank you for considering me for the position of floor manager. As you make your decision, I would like to highlight three items from my service and work record. First, in two years, I have not missed work and have been tardy only once, as the result of an accident. Second, my supervisors have given me the highest ratings on each of the monthly evaluations. Finally, I was pleased to have been given additional responsibilities during my supervisors' vacation times, and I learned a great deal about managing sales and accounts as a result. I welcome the challenge that would come with a promotion. Thank you again for your consideration.

Both writers highlight the same aspects of their employment records. Yet the first writer seems so full of himself that his superiors might wonder whether he has the people skills to be an effective supervisor. No one wants to work for a supervisor who is prone to such pronouncements as "responsibility is something to be treasured, not shirked." The other writer's just-the-facts approach is bound to make a better impression on the decision makers.

## *Avoid Cheap Emotion*

Avoid language that is full of sentimentality or cheap emotion. The following paragraph illustrates this error.

We were so deeply hurt by your cruel thoughtlessness in failing to introduce us to Jack Nicholson. He is the most wonderful, talented actor to have ever walked the face of the earth. My friend Charlotte and I so admire him and have ever since we can remember. Our admiration is a deep-channeled river that will never stop flowing. I'm sure you can imagine just how sorely disappointed and deeply wounded we were when we were not given the opportunity and honor to shake the hand and hear the voice of this great man. Neither I nor my dearest friend can seem to forget this slight, and I'm sure we will remain scarred for many years to come.

Instead of regretting not having introduced the writer to the great Jack Nicholson, the reader probably congratulates himself on not having let this nutcase get near him.

# Consistent Point of View

Authors can write using the first-person point of view (*I, me, we, us, my, our*), second-person point of view (*you, your*), or third-person point of view (*she, he, one, they, her, him, them, hers, his, one's, theirs*). Avoid switching points of view within or between sentences. Keep the point of view consistent throughout.

| INCONSISTENT | CONSISTENT |
|---|---|
| Citizens pay taxes, which entitles them [third person] to have some say in how their [third person] government is run. We [first person] have a right to insist on efficient use of our tax dollars. | We citizens pay taxes, which entitles us to have some say in how our government is run. We have a right to insist on efficient use of our tax dollars. |
| I [first person] enjoyed my trip to the park. You [second person] could see trees budding, flowers blooming, and squirrels running all over. | I enjoyed my trip to the park. I saw trees budding, flowers blooming, and squirrels running all over. |

## *Parallelism*

Two or more equivalent ideas in a sentence that have the same purpose should be presented in the same form. This is called *parallel structure.* Using parallel sentence structures not only helps your writing flow smoothly but also helps readers quickly recognize similar ideas. Look at the following examples of parallel words, phrases, and clauses.

| NOT PARALLEL | PARALLEL |
|---|---|
| My roommate is miserly, sloppy, and a bore. | My roommate is miserly, sloppy, and boring.<br>My roommate is a miser, a slob, and a bore. |
| My vacuum cleaner squealed loudly, shook violently, and dust filled the air. | My vacuum cleaner squealed loudly, shook violently, and filled the air with dust. |
| We soon discovered that our plane tickets were invalid, that our cruise reservations had never been made, and our travel agent left town. | We soon discovered that our plane tickets were invalid, that our cruise reservations had never been made, and that our travel agent had left town. |

Pairs of ideas should always be presented in parallel constructions. The following sentences present two or more equivalent ideas using similar forms.

> The committee finds no original and inspiring ideas in your proposal. What is original is not inspiring, and what is inspiring is not original.
> We came, we saw, we conquered.
> Belle was a timid, talented, and creative person.
> Ask not what your country can do for you; ask what you can do for your country.

## Practice 6: Using Parallel Structure

Rewrite the following sentence so that it has a parallel structure.

> As a result, some changes may occur in distribution, in accounting, human resources, or corporate.

# Using Gender-Neutral Language

It may seem that language is neutral, simply a tool for expressing ideas. Although this is partly true, our language reflects our values and communicates to others our social biases about gender and other issues. If a culture is gender biased, its language automatically becomes a vehicle for expressing and perpetuating those biases. One of the first steps toward overcoming such a prejudice is to examine the language and change it so that it no longer perpetuates false stereotypes about gender.

Some people resist changing their use of language, thinking that the words are harmless and that those who are offended are simply too sensitive. However, many readers are offended by the use of masculine pronouns to refer to both sexes or by diminutive suffixes indicating gender. Saying "Man must fulfill his destiny" or "Emily Dickinson was a great poetess" strikes them as archaic at best and insulting at worst.

## Gender Traps
The following are examples of language to avoid.

### Masculine Nouns or Pronouns
One serious difficulty comes when using pronouns. If the pronoun *he* is used to refer to an indefinite person—a teacher, a student, a postal carrier—the underlying assumption seems to be that all teachers or students or postal carriers are male. The same problem comes up with words such as *someone, somebody, everyone, no one,* or *nobody.* You can avoid offending readers unintentionally with gender-specific language in three ways: using gender-neutral terms, using the plural, or restructuring sentences altogether to avoid a gender reference.

Note that you cannot simply change the words *he* and *his* to *they* and *theirs.* "If a student wants to improve their test scores, they should good take notes and study" is grammatically incorrect. The pronouns *they* and *their* don't match their antecedent, *student*, in number, because *student* is singular and *they* is plural. An easy way to solve this is to make the antecedent plural: "If *students* want to improve their test scores, they should take good notes and study."

Here are some examples of gender traps in sentences and possible ways to revise them.

| GENDER-SPECIFIC | GENDER-NEUTRAL |
| --- | --- |
| The doctor uses his best judgment. | Doctors use their best judgment. |
| Every student must do his homework. | Students must do their homework. |
| A company executive is wise to choose his words carefully. | Company executives are wise to choose their words carefully. |
| If a manager wants respect, he should behave respectably. | Managers who want respect should behave respectably. |

You can avoid gender references altogether by restructuring your sentences. See how this is done in the following examples.

| GENDER-SPECIFIC | GENDER-NEUTRAL |
| --- | --- |
| A company executive is wise to drive himself relentlessly. | Anyone who desires success must work relentlessly. |
| A nurse must take her job seriously. | A nurse must take the job seriously. |
| Someone left his umbrella in the cloakroom. He should call Lost and Found. | The person who left an umbrella in the cloakroom should call Lost and Found. |

## Women as Subordinate to Men

Writers can make it seem as if men are always leaders and women are always subordinate in many subtle ways.

| POOR | BETTER |
|------|--------|
| A principal and his staff need to establish good communication. | The principal and staff need to establish good communication. |
| If you ask the nurse, she will summon the doctor if he is available. | If you ask, a nurse will summon an available doctor. |
| Bob took his wife and children to a movie. | Bob and Mary took their children to a movie. |
| Emil asked his secretary to check the mail. | Emil asked the secretary to check the mail. |

Writers also fall into a similar trap when they refer to men according to their abilities, while referring to women according to their appearances.

| POOR | BETTER |
|------|--------|
| Dr. Routmeir and his attractive, blond wife arrived at the party at 9:00 P.M. | Dr. and Ms. Routmeir arrived at the party at 9:00 P.M. Herman and Betty Routmeir arrived at the party at 9:00 P.M. |
| The talented violinist and his beautiful accompanist took the stage. | The violinist and the accompanist took the stage. |

Note that in both sentences in the left column, the man is referred to by his profession, while the woman is referred to by her appearance. To avoid this, refer to both in the same context, either physical or professional. Furthermore, in the first example, the man is addressed by a formal title and the woman is not identified except as the wife belonging to the man. To avoid this, refer to both by name.

### "Men's" Jobs and "Women's" Jobs

Avoid making special note of gender when discussing a job traditionally done by men or women—those traditions don't hold anymore! In the following examples, the first sentence makes traditional assumptions, while the second does not:

> When a man on board collapsed, a lady pilot emerged
>     from the cockpit and a male nurse offered assistance.
> When a passenger collapsed, a pilot emerged from the
>     cockpit and a nurse offered assistance.

The references *lady pilot* and *male nurse* call attention to themselves because they assume that the reader will automatically assign a gender to the job. Readers may be offended by this assumption.

### Gender-Specific Terms

There are a lot of words in English that traditionally have taken different forms for male and female persons. These distinctions are becoming obsolete. Today, most people prefer one term to refer to both men and women in their particular roles. This change doesn't have to be awkward, as you can see in the following table.

In the past, it was common to use the word *man* to refer to all humans, both male and female. Today, that usage will offend many readers. The following sentences demonstrate this kind of usage and a more appropriate alternative.

> If man wishes to improve his environment, he must
>     improve himself.
> If humanity wishes to improve its environment, each
>     individual must improve.

The following table lists some common gender-specific terms and good alternatives.

| GENDER-SPECIFIC | GENDER-NEUTRAL |
| --- | --- |
| waiter, waitress | server |
| stewardess, steward | flight attendant |
| policeman, policewoman | police officer |
| chairwoman, chairman | chairperson, chair |
| man-made | synthetic, artificial |
| foreman | supervisor |
| manpower | employees, personnel |
| man, mankind | humans, people |

# Practice 7:
# Using Gender-Neutral Language

Rewrite the following sentences so that they use gender-neutral language.

1. A presidential candidate must realize that his life is no longer his own.
2. If an mailman wishes to change his route, he must speak with his supervisor, who will tell him how to proceed.
3. If anyone wants to improve his commissions, he should increase his sales.

## ⇨ TIP

Pay close attention to the tone and style of everything you write. Is the degree of formality appropriate for the message and the audience? Do you sense emotional overload? Is the point of view consistent? Are equivalent ideas presented equally? Does the writing contain gender references? If so, are they likely to offend the reader?

# Answers

## *Practice 1: Eliminating Redundancy*

**1.** We are pleased to announce the opening of Succasunna's new Municipal Park playground. (Answers will vary.)

**2.** Using computers can save time and money. (Answers will vary.)

**3.** I let my supervisor beat me at golf so she would promote me. (Answers will vary.)

## *Practice 2: Eliminating Passive Voice*

**1.** The committee denied your grant because it did not follow the application guidelines.

**2.** The Board of Directors accepted the resignation.

## *Practice 3: Eliminating Cliché*

When it comes to fixing our nation's energy crisis, we need to think outside the box. We will need to roll up our sleeves and dig in, finding ways to reduce our current energy footprints while developing alternative forms of energy. Children are our future, and if we deplete this planet and leave them with no resources, we leave them up the creek without a paddle. Sustainability studies and research can show us the writing on the wall and highlight areas where we can be more "green" as a society. Information is our friend as we look to conserve, create, and maintain resources for a brighter tomorrow.

## *Practice 4: Clear and Concise Writing*

**1.** a

**2.** b

**3.** b

**4.** a

## *Practice 5: Avoiding Colloquialism*

Hey boss,

The presentation for tomorrow's meeting is ready. Fred and I were hanging out late last night, pulling together our research and our ideas so we could whip them into shape. After we were done, I emailed the dude over in the graphics department to finish the formatting. This morning, I eyeballed the information to make sure everything was included, and I think we're good to go. Lemme know if there's anything else you'd like me to do before tomorrow's meeting.

## *Practice 6: Using Parallel Structure*

As a result, some changes may occur in distribution, accounting, human resources, or corporate. *Or* As a result, some changes may occur in distribution, in accounting, in human resources, or in corporate.

## *Practice 7: Using Gender-Neutral Language*

1. Presidential candidates must realize that their lives are no longer their own.
2. Postal carriers who wish to change their routes should speak with their supervisor, who will explain how to proceed.
3. Anyone who wants to improve his or her commissions should increase sales.

# Commonly Confused Words

**T**hrew or through? To, two, or too? Brake or break? This chapter reviews a host of words that are often confused with other words and shows you when to use them. If you learn to distinguish these words, you will avoid errors in your writing.

## Accept/Except/Expect

- **Accept** is a verb meaning *receive, bear.*
- **Except** is a preposition meaning *but, excluding.*
- **Expect** is a verb meaning *anticipate, demand, assume.*
  **Examples:**
  This client **expects** (*demands*) nothing **except** (*but*) the most sophisticated options available.
  Will you **accept** (*bear*) the responsibility for this decision?
  We **expect** (*anticipate*) everyone to come **except** (*excluding*) John.

## *Advice/Advise*

- **Advice** is a noun meaning *suggestion* or *suggestions*. It rhymes with *ice*. (Hint: Think *advICE*.)
- **Advise** is a verb meaning *suggest to*, *warn*. It rhymes with *wise*.
  **Examples:**
  We **advise** (*suggest to*) you to proceed carefully.
  That was the best **advice** (*suggestion*) I've received so far.

## *Affect/Effect*

- **Affect** is a verb meaning *alter*, *inspire* or *move emotionally*, *imitate*. **Affected**, besides being the past tense of *affect*, can also be used as an adjective meaning *imitated*, *pretentious*. **Affect** is also a noun referring to *feeling* or *emotion*.
- **Effect** as a noun means *consequence*. As a verb, it means *cause*.
  **Examples:**
  How will this plan **affect** (*alter*) our jobs? What **effect** (*consequence*) will this restructuring have on profits? Will it **effect** (*cause*) an increase?
  The movie **affected** (*moved emotionally*) Marian.
  He **affected** (*imitated*) an English accent.
  The **affected** (*pretentious*) speech fooled no one.

## *Already/All Ready*

- **Already** is an adverb meaning *as early as this*, *previously*, or *by this time*.
- **All ready** means *completely ready* or *totally ready*.
  **Examples:**
  At age four, Brigitta is reading **already** (*as early as this*).
  We had **already** (*previously*, *by this time*) finished.
  Are we **all ready** (*completely ready*) to go?

## Altogether/All Together

- **Altogether** is an adverb meaning *entirely, completely.*
- **All together** means *simultaneously.*
  **Examples:**
  These claims are **altogether** (*entirely*) false.
  The audience responded **all together** (*simultaneously*).

## Alot/Allot/A Lot

- **Alot.** There's no such word as *alot.*
- **Allot** means *to portion out* something.
- **A lot** is a noun that means a *large number* or *many.*
  **Example:**
  I thought it was all right that we **allotted** (portioned out) tickets to **a lot** (many) of our best customers.

## Brake/Break

- **Brake** as a verb means *slow* or *stop.* As a noun, it refers to a device for slowing or stopping motion.
- **Break** as a verb means *separate, shatter,* or *adjourn.* As a noun, it means *separation, crack, pause,* or *opportunity.*
  **Examples:**
  During our **break** (*pause*), we spotted a **break** (*crack*) in the pipeline.
  **Brake** (*slow*) gently when driving on ice by applying slight pressure to the **brake** (*drag*).

## By/Buy

- **By** is a preposition used to introduce a phrase (*by the book, by the time, by the way*).
- **Buy** as a verb means *purchase.* As a noun, it means *bargain, deal.*
  **Examples:**
  We stopped **by** (*preposition*) the office supply store to **buy** (*purchase*) some printer ink.
  That real estate was a great **buy** (*deal*).

## Capital/Capitol

- **Capital** as a noun means either *assets* or *the city that is the seat of government*. As an adjective, it means *main, very important*, or *deserving of death.*
- **Capitol** is a noun referring to the building that houses the government.

  **Examples:**

  How much **capital** (*assets*) are you willing to invest?

  I think that's a **capital** (*main*) objective.

  Some states consider first-degree murder a **capital** (*deserving of death*) crime.

  Albany is the **capital** (*city*) of New York.

  No legislators were injured in the explosion in the **capitol** (*building*).

## Choose/Chose

- **Choose** is a verb meaning *select*. It rhymes with *bruise.*
- **Chose** is past tense of choose; it means *selected*. It rhymes with *hose.*

  **Example:**

  Henry **chose** (*selected*) flex hours on Friday afternoons. I will **choose** (*select*) the same option.

## Dear/Deer

- **Dear** is an adjective meaning *valued, loved.*
- **Deer** is a noun referring to a four-legged animal that lives in the woods.

  **Example:**

  His **dear** (*loved*) daughter's favorite movie is *Bambi*, about a **deer** (*animal*).

## Die/Dye

- **Die** is a verb meaning *pass away, fade.*
- **Dye** as a verb means *to color, tint*. As a noun, it refers to coloring or pigment.

**Example:**

They waited for the wind to **die** (*fade*) before they decided to **dye** (*color*) the sheets.

## Everyday/Every Day

- **Everyday** is an adjective meaning *ordinary, usual.*
- **Every day** means *each day.*

**Examples:**

These are our **everyday** (*usual*) low prices.

The associates sort the merchandise **every day** (*each day*).

## Hear/Here

- **Hear** is a verb meaning *listen to.*
- **Here** is an adverb meaning *in this place, to this place.*

**Example:**

Please gather **here** (*to this place*) so you can **hear** (*listen to*) the director's announcement.

## Hole/Whole

- **Hole** is a noun meaning *opening, gap.*
- **Whole** as an adjective means *entire, intact.* As a noun, it means *entire part or amount.*

**Examples:**

The **whole** (*entire*) group heard the message.

They patched the **hole** (*opening*) in the wall.

## Knew/New

- **Knew** is a verb, the past tense of *know.* It means *understood, recognized.*
- **New** is an adjective meaning *fresh, different, current.*

**Example:**

I **knew** (*understood*) they were planning to hire a **new** (*different*) developer.

## Know/No

- **Know** is a verb meaning *understand, recognize.*
- **No** as an adverb means *not so, not at all.* As an adjective, it means *none, not one.*

  **Example:**

  As far as I **know** (*understand*), we have **no** (*not one*) meetings scheduled on Tuesday.

## Lead/Led/Lead

- **Lead** as a verb means *guide, direct.* As a noun, it means *front position.* It rhymes with *seed.*
- **Led** as a verb is the past tense of **lead**, meaning *guided, directed.* It rhymes with *red.*
- **Lead** is a noun that is the name of a metal. It rhymes with *red.*

  **Examples:**

  Geronimo **led** (*guided*) the small band to safety.

  We hope the next elected officials will **lead** (*guide*) us to economic recovery.

  A pound of styrofoam weighs as much as a pound of **lead** (*the metal*).

  Jake took the **lead** (*front position*) as the group headed out of town.

## Loose/Lose/Loss

- **Loose** is an adjective meaning *free, unrestrained, not tight.* It rhymes with *goose.*
- **Lose** is a verb meaning *misplace, to be defeated, fail to keep.* It rhymes with *shoes.*
- **Loss** is a noun meaning *defeat* or *downturn.* It rhymes with *toss.*

  **Examples:**

  The chickens ran **loose** (*free*) on the farm.

  The knot holding the boat to the dock was **loose** (*not tight*).

Where did the customer **lose** (*misplace*) his gloves?

The investors will **lose** (*fail to keep*) considerable capital if the market suffers a **loss** (*downturn*).

## Maybe/May Be

- **Maybe** is an adverb meaning *perhaps*.
- **May be** is a verb phrase meaning *might be*.

**Example:**

**Maybe** (*perhaps*) the next batch will be better than this one. On the other hand, it **may be** (*might be*) worse.

## Meat/Meet

- **Meat** is a noun meaning *edible flesh*, *edible part*, or *essence*.
- **Meet** as a verb means *assemble, greet, fulfill*. As a noun, it means *assembly*.

**Examples:**

Before a track **meet** (*assembly*), it is better to eat foods high in carbohydrates rather than **meat** (*flesh*).

The **meat** (*essence*) of the letter explains that our efforts did not **meet** (*fulfill*) his standards.

## One/Won

- **One** can be an adjective meaning *single*. It can also be a noun used to mean *a single person or thing*.
- **Won** is a verb, the past tense of *win*. It means *prevailed, achieved, acquired*.

**Example:**

Jacquez is the **one** (*noun referring to* Jacquez) who **won** (*achieved*) the office raffle this year.

## Passed/Past

- **Passed** is a verb, the past tense of *pass*, meaning *transferred, went ahead* or *by, elapsed, finished*.
- **Past** as a noun means *history*. As an adjective, it means *former*. As an adverb, it means *by* or *beyond*.

**Examples:**

The first runner **passed** (*transferred*) the baton to the second just as she **passed** (*went by*) the stands. Three seconds **passed** (*elapsed*) before the next runner came by.

Harriet **passed** (*finished*) her bar exam on the first try.

I managed a team of freelancers in my **past** (*former*) position.

Avoid digging up the **past** (*history*) if you can.

Nathan walks **past** (*by*) the mailroom every day.

## Peace/Piece

- **Peace** is a noun meaning *tranquility*.
- **Piece** as a noun means *division, creation*. As a verb, it means *patch, repair*.

**Example:**

If you can **piece** (*patch*) together the **pieces** (*bits*) of this story, perhaps we can have some **peace** (*tranquility*) around here.

## Personal/Personnel

- **Personal** is an adjective meaning *private*.
- **Personnel** as a noun means *staff, employees* and as an adjective means *dealing with staff or employees*.

**Example:**

The director of **personnel** (*staff*) keeps all the **personnel** (*employee*) files in order and guards any **personal** (*private*) information they contain.

## Plain/Plane

- **Plain** as an adjective means *ordinary, clear, simple*. As a noun, it refers to flat country, also sometimes written as **plains**.
- **Plane** is a noun meaning *airship* or *flat surface*. It is occasionally used as a verb or adjective meaning *level*.
  **Examples:**
  They wore **plain** (*ordinary*) clothes.
  It was **plain** (*clear*) to see.
  The meal we ate on the **plains** (*flat country*) was quite
     **plain** (*simple*).

## Principal/Principle

- **Principal** as a noun means *the head of a school* or *an investment*. As an adjective, it means *primary, major*.
- **Principle** is a noun meaning *rule, law, belief*.
  **Examples:**
  The **principal** (*head*) of Calbert High School used the **principal** (*investment*) of an endowment fund to cover this
  month's salaries.
  The **principal** (*primary*) objective is to make decisions that
  are in keeping with our **principles** (*beliefs*).

## Quite/Quit/Quiet

- **Quite** is an adverb meaning *completely, very, entirely*. It rhymes with *fight*.
- **Quit** is a verb meaning *stop, cease* (present tense) or *stopped, ceased* (past tense). It rhymes with *sit*.
- **Quiet** as an adjective means *calm, silent, noiseless*. As a verb, it means *soothe, calm*. As a noun, it means *tranquility, peacefulness*. It almost rhymes with *riot*.
  **Example:**
  The firm was **quite** (*very*) surprised when its most productive investment specialist **quit** (*stopped*) work and
  opted for the **quiet** (*calm*) life of a monk.

### Right/Write/Rite

- **Right** is an adjective meaning *correct*, *proper*, or *opposite of left*.
- **Write** is a verb meaning *record*, *inscribe*.
- **Rite** is a noun meaning *ceremony*, *ritual*.
  **Example:**
  I will **write** (*record*) the exact procedures so you will be able to perform the **rite** (*ceremony*) in the **right** (*proper*) way.

### Scene/Seen

- **Scene** is a noun meaning *view*, *site*, or *commotion*.
- **Seen** is a verb, the past participle of *see*, meaning *observed*, *noticed*.
  **Example:**
  There was quite a **scene** (*commotion*) at the **scene** (*site*) of the accident. It was the worst the town had ever **seen** (*observed*).

### Seam/Seem

- **Seam** is a noun meaning *joint*, *joining point*.
- **Seem** is a verb meaning *appear*.
  **Example:**
  Does it **seem** (*appear*) as if this **seam** (*joint*) is weakening?

### Sent/Cent/Scent

- **Sent** is a verb, the past tense of *send*. It means *dispatched*, *transmitted*.
- **Cent** is a noun meaning *one penny*, a coin worth .01 of a dollar.
- **Scent** is a noun meaning *odor*, *smell*.

**Example:**
For a mere **cent** (*penny*), I bought an envelope perfumed with the **scent** (*odor*) of jasmine, which I **sent** (*dispatched*) to my grandmother.

### Sight/Site/Cite

- **Sight** as a noun means *ability to see*. As a verb, it means *see, spot*.
- **Site** is a noun meaning *location, position*.
- **Cite** is a verb meaning *quote, make reference to*.
  **Examples:**
  The editor's **sight** (*ability to see*) was acute enough to **sight** (*spot*) even the smallest printing error.
  This is the proposed **site** (*location*) for the new building.
  You must **cite** (*make reference to*) the source of your information.

### Suppose/Supposed

- **Suppose** is a verb meaning *assume, imagine*.
- **Supposed** as a verb is the past tense of *suppose* and means *assumed, imagined*. As an adjective, it means *expected, obligated*.
  **Examples:**
  I **suppose** (*assume*) you'll be late, as usual.
  We all **supposed** (*assumed*) you would be late.
  You were **supposed** (*expected*) to have picked up the copies of the report before you came to the meeting.

### Than/Then

- **Than** is a conjunctive word used to make a comparison.
- **Then** is an adverb telling when or meaning *next*.
  **Example:**
  **Then** (*next*) the group discussed the ways in which the new procedures worked better **than** (*conjunction making a comparison*) the old procedures.

## *Threw/Through*

- **Threw** is a verb, the past tense of *throw*, meaning *tossed.*
- **Through** is an adverb or a preposition meaning *in one side and out the other.* Use **through** to introduce a prepositional phrase: *through the door, through the lobby, through the mist.*

  **Example:**

  Fred **threw** (*tossed*) the ball **through** (*in one side and out the other*) the hoop.

## *To/Too/Two*

- **To** is a preposition or part of an infinitive. Use **to** to introduce a prepositional phrase: *to the store, to the top, to his laboratory, to our advantage, to an open door,* etc. Or use **to** as an infinitive (*to* followed by a verb, sometimes separated by adverbs): *to run, to seek, to propose, to write, to explode, to badly botch, to carefully examine,* etc.
- **Too** is an adverb meaning *also, very.*
- **Two** is an adjective, the name of a number, as in *one, two, three.*

  **Example:**

  The couple went **to** (*preposition*) the deli **to** (*infinitive*) pick up **two** (*the number*) dinners because both of them were **too** (*very*) tired **to** (*infinitive*) cook.

## *Use/Used/Used to*

- **Use** as a verb means *utilize, deplete.* It rhymes with *lose.* As a noun, it rhymes with *goose* and means *purpose.*
- **Used** as a verb is the past tense of *use* and means *utilized, depleted.* As an adjective, it means *secondhand.*

- **Used to** can be used as an adjective, meaning *accustomed to*, or as an adverb meaning *formerly*. (Note: Never write *use to* when you mean *accustomed to* or *formerly*.)

  **Examples:**

  Just **use** (*utilize*) the same password we **used** (*utilized*) yesterday.

  What's the **use** (*purpose*) of trying yet another time?

  We should consider buying **used** (*secondhand*) equipment.

  We **used to** (*formerly*) require a second opinion.

  Residents of Buffalo, New York, are **used to** (*accustomed to*) cold temperatures.

## Weak/Week

- **Weak** is an adjective meaning *flimsy*, *frail*, or *powerless*.
- **Week** is a noun meaning *a period of seven days*.

  **Example:**

  The company's sales figures for the previous **week** (*seven days*) were very **weak** (*frail*).

## Weather/Whether

- **Weather** is a noun referring to the condition outside.
- **Whether** is an adverb used when referring to a possibility.

  **Examples:**

  The **weather** (*condition outside*) took a turn for the worse.

  Let me know **whether** (*a possibility*) you are interested in this new system.

## Where/Wear/Were

- **Where** is an adverb referring to *place*, *location*.
- **Wear** as a verb means *put on* or *tire*. As a noun, it means *deterioration*.
- **Were** is a verb, the plural past tense of *be*.

**Examples:**

The checks **were** (*form of* be) put in the mail yesterday.

The tires showed excessive **wear** (*deterioration*).

They will **wear** (*tire*) out these shoes if they **wear** (*put on*) them too much.

**Where** (*location*) are the clothes you **were** (*form of be*) planning to **wear** (*put on*) tomorrow?

## Which/Witch

- **Which** is a pronoun dealing with choice. As an adverb, it introduces a subordinate clause.
- **Witch** is a noun meaning *sorceress, enchantress.*

**Examples:**

**Which** (*choice*) one do you want?

This car, **which** (*introduces subordinate clause*) I have never driven, is the one I'm thinking about buying.

I don't know **which** (*choice*) **witch** (*enchantress*) is most popular for children's Halloween costumes.

# Practice: Easily Confused Words

Circle the correct word in the parentheses.

**1.** When you (right, write, rite) the final report, please be sure you use the (right, write, rite) statistics.

**2.** If you (quite, quit, quiet) talking for a minute and give us some (quite, quit, quiet), I will be (quite, quit, quiet) happy to ask the others to maintain this (quite, quit, quiet) atmosphere for the duration of the meeting.

**3.** The researcher asked permission to (sight, site, cite) my study in his report.

**4.** When she saw the biker ahead (brake, break), Sally slammed on her (brakes, breaks) to avoid the (brake, break) in the concrete path.

**5.** The (scene, seen) at the Grand Canyon was breathtaking. Have you (scene, seen) it before?

**6.** The private (plain, plane) had a (plain, plane) tan interior.

**7.** There (maybe, may be) more storms tomorrow, so (maybe, may be) we should plan to hold the reception indoors.

**8.** If you had been (already, all ready), we could have (already, all ready) begun.

**9.** Would you run (by, buy) the post office to (by, buy) some stamps?

**10.** I can (hear, here) the speaker much better now that I am sitting (hear, here).

**11.** I didn't (know, no) that that you had (know, no) idea how to get to the conference center.

**12.** The marketing (one, won) the client over in under (one, won) hour.

**13.** Ms. Wallace interviewed each candidate twice to (choose, chose) the best person for the job.

**14.** After the (loose, lose, loss) of her job, she began to (loose, lose, loss) confidence.

**15.** It's 7:30; aren't you (suppose, supposed) to be at the airport by 8:00?

**16.** I waited until I'd collected more (then, than) enough donations, and (then, than) I contacted the director of the homeless shelter.

**17.** (Accept, Except, Expect) for Mr. Nelson, Ms. Lawrence didn't (accept, except, expect) anyone else to (accept, except, expect) the committee's costly construction proposal.

**18.** The new work schedule (affected, effected) production in a positive way.

**19.** The (personnel, personal) information you submit to (personnel, personal) will be kept strictly confidential.

**20.** The employees' (principal, principle) concern is workload.

## Answers

1. write, right
2. quit, quiet, quite, quiet
3. cite
4. brake, brake, break
5. scene, seen
6. plane, plain
7. may be, maybe
8. all ready, already
9. by, buy
10. hear, here
11. know, no
12. won, one
13. choose
14. loss, lose
15. supposed
16. than, then
17. except, expect, accept
18. affected
19. personal, personnel
20. principal

# Section 3:
# Workplace Writing

I n today's workplace, where less and less business is conducted face to face, it remains highly advantageous to know how to write well. This section teaches you how to build the scaffolding necessary to create a powerful and effective business letter—a letter that will get the results you are looking for. It also covers electronic correspondence (a topic that has become worthy of a book in itself), memos, and documents for meeting and presentations. You will find a wide variety of real-world sample communications that you can draw upon for all your professional work. They provide a useful overall picture of what your finished product should look like.

If you apply all that you have learned from this section when writing your own communications, you should be writing successfully in no time!

# 5 Traditional Letters

**Y**ou can organize different types of letters in different ways, but following a logical order and getting to the point are imperative to being clear and understood, no matter what type of letter you are writing. Say what you want to say, support it with facts, be specific, ask for what you need, thank the reader, and then end the letter.

Traditional letters traditionally consist of the following elements, in this order:

- **Your return address.** Omit this if your letter will be printed on company letterhead that includes the company's address.
- **The date on which you're writing your letter.** This should be fully spelled out. For instance: *December 5, 2015*

- **The name and address of the person you are writing to.**
  Include the person's job title, if you know it, and company name. For instance:
  *Jane Smith*
  *Marketing Director*
  *Teapots Inc.*
  *201 N. Harrington Road*
  *St. Louis, MO 63101*
- **The salutation.** This is your opening or greeting and usually begins with "Dear," followed by the person's name, followed by a colon. It's also acceptable to use a comma in place of the colon, although it may be considered less formal. For instance:
  *Dear Ms. Jones:*
  *Dear Hillary,*

Generally, don't address the recipient by his or her first name unless you're already acquainted. However, if the person has signed correspondence with a first name, it's fine to take your cue from that and respond in kind. Remember, when using last names, use the neutral term "Ms." for women rather than "Miss" or "Mrs.," which assume information about a woman's marital status.

- **The body of the letter.** This is the "meat" of the letter itself.
- **The closing.** This is usually a few short words directly above your signature, followed by a comma, such as:
  *Sincerely,*
  *Warm regards,*
- **Your signature, name, and title.**

These elements should begin four to six lines from the top of the page. All of the elements above should be left justified, with one line space between each. Another option many people choose is to center the date and the "signature block" (your closing, signature, name, and title).

Put one to two line spaces between the return address, the date, the recipient's address, and the salutation. Use one line space between each paragraph of your letter, as well as above and below your signature block.

Take a look at this sample letter.

---

Penelope Morris
53 Northwoods Lane
San Diego, CA 92105

**(Skip 4 lines)**

January 7, 2015

**(Skip 2-3 lines)**

Benjamin Brown
President
Brown Productions
2105 George Mason Drive
La Jolla, CA 92037

Dear Mr. Brown:
Thank you so much for speaking with me last week. It's a pleasure to be working with your firm to plan our second annual fundraising dinner.

Enclosed please find our 50% deposit and signed contract. If you need anything else from me before we get started, please let me know.

Sincerely,

**(Skip 3 lines)**

*Penelope Morris*

Penelope Morris
Chair
San Diego Garden Club

---

# Introductory Letter

One type of letter you might write is an introductory letter. The purpose of an introductory letter is to introduce yourself or your business, generally to a potential client. Because this letter is often the first contact between you and the other party, it's important to make a good impression.

An effective introductory letter should:

- **Be direct and to the point.** Because the other party doesn't know you yet, he or she will want to quickly understand why you are writing and what next steps you're proposing. Be clear and concise, and limit the letter to one page.
- **Open with who you are.** Your first paragraph should introduce yourself and explain why you're writing.
- **Explain the benefit to the recipient.** Your second paragraph should explain the potential benefits to the recipient of using your services. You might mention specifics here that will make your service more enticing, such as the quality of the service or product you offer and any special discounts.
- **Clearly suggest next steps.** Always end by clearly stating what you would like to happen next. You might ask that the recipient call you or visit your website for more information, or you might note that you will call to follow up in one week.

Here's an example of what an introductory letter might look like. Note that it's short and direct, is clear about the benefits the writer is offering, and closes by suggesting next steps.

Ed Jones
Colewood Marketing
10501 Johnson Parkway
Washington, DC 20035

June 15, 2015

*(Always include the company name if you know it.)*

Karen Mitchell
Hats Emporium
521 Oak Street
Washington, DC 20007

Dear Ms. Mitchell:

*(State your purpose for writing up front in your first paragraph.)*

I'm writing to introduce myself and my company, Colewood Marketing. I'd love to see if we can help you with your website and online marketing.

*(Always explain the benefit you can offer to the recipient.)*

We've worked with many companies your size and helped them see significant growth in web traffic and online sales, often in just a few months. The majority of our work is repeat business because our clients are so happy with the results we get for them. Additionally, we're offering a special 15% discount on any services you sign up for this month, so this would be a great time to explore what we can do for you.

*(Clearly suggest next steps to close out your letter.)*

I'd love to talk with you more and see how we might help. I'll give you a call next week and see if we can arrange a time to meet.

Sincerely,

*Ed Jones*

Ed Jones
Senior Sales Representative
Colewood Marketing

### *Remember, Clarity is Key*

You never want your reader to wonder about *any* key details after reading your correspondence. Here are some sentences that leave the reader guessing, followed by examples of how to be specific:

**Vague:** *I hope to meet with you again soon!*
**Clear/Specific:** *We are looking forward to an answer about the contract by January 4.*

**Vague:** *We greatly appreciated your help with the Randolph matter. You are a great new asset to our team.*
**Clear/Specific:** *Your decision to renegotiate the Randolph contract earned us an additional $10,000. Pam and Ronan tell us you are the best new attorney on staff.*

**Vague:** *Your investment should increase significantly by next year.*
**Clear/Specific:** *Your investment should increase 20% by next year.*

**Vague:** *The new system has been very profitable.*
**Clear/Specific:** *The new system has reduced operating costs by 30%.*

**Vague:** *We're running somewhat behind schedule.*
**Clear/Specific:** *We're running one week late.*

# Inquiry Letter

In an inquiry letter, the order of the information should be as follows:

- what you want
- who you are and why you are asking for it
- brief thank you to end it

Remember that the reader is most interested in the gist of your letter. You will come across as a straight shooter, someone who is interested in what matters most, if you write in that order.

Carrie Grove
90 Berry Street, #1R
Brooklyn, NY 11211

September 22, 2015

Ms. Delano
85 Skyler Street
Syracuse, NY 13215

Dear Ms. Delano,

I am a freelance photographer working for *Introspection* magazine, and I am writing to ask if you might be available for a portrait sitting sometime in the next two weeks. The publication would like your interview with journalist Brad Husted to be accompanied by a photograph. If this idea suits you, please let me know dates and times when you might be available.

Thank you in advance. I look forward to meeting you.

Sincerely,
*Carrie Grove*
Portrait Photographer

# Thank You Letter

Thank you letters are a great way to show your appreciation and improve relationships with your manager, coworkers, clients, and others in your professional network. Taking the time to write thank you can be a meaningful gesture that builds the relationship and ensures that you'll continue to receive help (or business) in the future.

Following are some of the situations in which you might send a thank you letter:

- to thank a client for his or her business
- to thank a business contact for referring a client to you
- to thank a colleague for above-and-beyond assistance with an important project
- to thank a manager for mentoring you
- to thank a vendor for providing excellent service
- or in any other situation where you want to express appreciation

## Key Elements of a Thank You Letter

To make your thank you letter as effective as possible, follow these steps.

- **Make it personal.** Your words should make it clear that this is a personal note of thanks, not a generic form letter that you're sending to many people. Open with the recipient's name, and include specific details about why you're grateful.

- **Clearly state what you are thanking the person for—** whether it is choosing your business or staying late to get an important mailing out for you.
- **Don't make a sales pitch.** A thank you letter should be solely about expressing thanks; if you include a sales pitch, the thank you will seem disingenuous.
- **Keep it short.** A thank you should be no longer than a page and generally just two to three paragraphs.

### TIP

While it's fine type a thank you letter on letterhead, many people prefer to handwrite a note on a card for a more personal touch.

Here's an example of a thank you letter. Note that it has a friendly and personal tone, is specific about what the writer is grateful for, and is short and to the point.

Linda Garcia
Northwest Association of Printers
564 Carolina St., #2
Portland, OR 97217

February 1, 2015

Paul Adams
The Perfect Event
717 Watson Parkway
Cedar Mill, OR 97229

Dear Paul,

Thank you so much for your assistance in planning our winter conference. You were invaluable to us during a hectic time, and the event's success was a tribute to your organizational skills, savvy negotiating, and incredible eye for detail. You were right—those goody bags were a hit!

I know how much work you put into the event, well beyond what was originally envisioned, and I'm so grateful for all you did. It was a true pleasure working with you!

Sincerely,

*Linda Garcia*

Linda Garcia
Owner
Northside Printing

# 6 Emails

**E**mail, which at its inception seemed best used like a telegram—short, concise messages, containing abbreviations and sometimes only lowercase letters—is now used to communicate just about anything to anyone for any reason. For example, in business, emails are used to apply for employment, to write a thank you note, to distribute meeting minutes, to request vacation time, to communicate in a collective setting, to hold individual exchanges, to place an order, to generate a receipt, to provide product support, and for myriad other uses that were once achieved primarily through telephone calls, face-to-face interactions, and the postal service.

While it may be second nature for you to shoot off quick emails to colleagues, it is very important to put thought into how you structure and compose them, or you may end up communicating messages you never intended. In this chapter, we'll explore how to use email effectively and professionally.

# To, Cc, and Bcc

Each email message has a header, which is divided into fields: To, From, Cc, Bcc, Subject, and Date. The Date and the From fields are filled in automatically, but you fill in the rest of the fields.

Usually, the very first thing you type in an email is the **To** field. Filling it out correctly might seem obvious, but it's important to be thoughtful about who you send your message to. Too often, people overfill this line, sending their message to anyone and everyone they can think of, just in case. But this can annoy others and dilute the impact of your message. (If you've ever watched your mailbox fill up with emails that had nothing to do with you, you'll understand this!)

**Cc** stands for "carbon copy." It stems from the days when type-writers were used to write letters. Someone sending a postal letter might have used carbon paper to make a copy to send to someone else, in order to avoid having to type the letter twice.

The Cc field is useful when you want someone to be aware of your message but don't expect a reply because the person isn't directly involved. The Cc field can be used to keep other people in the loop. For example, you might Cc your boss on an email to a vendor to keep her in the loop and let her know that you're on top of your project. The email is directed to the vendor, but your boss receives it, too.

**Bcc** stands for "blind carbon copy" and lets you hide certain recipients. If you put recipients in the Bcc field, they will receive your message but others copied on the message will not be able to see who your Bcc'd recipients are (or even that you have any Bcc'd recipients).

In general, it's considered poor etiquette to Bcc people in order to conceal from your main recipient that you are sharing the email with others. However, the Bcc field is useful if you are sending an email to multiple people and don't want to share their email addresses with each other. For instance, if you are sending an invitation to a reception to multiple clients, you may choose to protect your clients' privacy by including everyone in the Bcc field.

| |
|---|
| **To:** People required to take action |
| **Cc:** People you want to keep informed but who are not your primary recipients |
| **Bcc:** People who will receive the message without any of the other recipients knowing; also useful for larger emailings |

Look at the following example.

> **To:** *Janet Hudson, Juan Garcia*
> **Cc:** *Melody Smith*
> **Bcc:** *Bob Washington*

All the recipients of this email will see the following header information when they receive the email:

> **To:** *Janet Hudson, Juan Garcia*
> **Cc:** *Melody Smith*

Janet, Juan, and Melody will not know that Bob was Bcc'd. Bob will realize that he was Bcc'd, but he won't know if anyone else was Bcc'd.

Think carefully about who needs to receive your message and stick just to that group. Be very very careful about "replying all" to an email, particularly when others may have been Bcc'd. If your office uses listservs (a macro shortcut that allows you to email your entire department or possibly the entire company with just a few key strokes), be especially wary of how you reply to it.

# Subject Lines

Good subject lines are short, concise, to the point, and accurate. By reading the subject line, your recipient should be able to tell what your message will be about. A good subject line also makes it easier to locate the message later.

### Be Concise
The subject line should only be a few words, not a lengthy sentence.

> **Good:** *Meeting Friday 8/25 at 2:00*
> **Bad:** *Let's meet at 2:00 Friday in the 3rd floor conference room to talk about the new fall line and any other topics you want to add to the agenda.*

### Don't Be Vague
Overly general subject lines won't help your recipient know what you're writing about.

> **Good:** *Emily's upcoming performance review*
> **Bad:** *Emily*

### Use Subject Lines with Meaning
Avoid subject lines that don't explain why you're writing.

> **Good:** *New procedure for ordering supplies*
> **Bad:** *Hi*
> **Bad:** *Message from Jason*

### *Changing the Subject Line*

Sometimes after several replies in a chain of email, the topic will change. The original email might have been about a new research finding, but after some back and forth, you end up discussing an upcoming board meeting. When this happens, change the subject line accordingly, so that it reflects the content of the new emails.

**Original Subject Line:** *New finding in Lab A*
**New Subject Line:** *Topics for 3/12 board meeting*

Changing the subject line will allow both you and your correspondent to find the email more easily later without having to search through every message that the two of you sent.

## Formatting

The basic elements that open a traditional letter (date, address, etc.) are already programmed into the header information in your email, so you don't need to type them out in the body of the email message itself. Instead, you'll start with the salutation, such as "Dear Jane."

The basic elements of an email are:

- Header information (does not appear in the email message body)
- Salutation or opening
- Message body
- Closing and signature line

Here's an example of what this looks like all pulled together.

From: Michelle Marlow
Date: June 21, 2015
To: Jerry Wolff
CC: Melissa Martinez
Subject: website proposal

*(The salutation here is informal because there's already an established relationship.)*

Hi Jerry,

Thanks so much for sending me the proposal for managing our website. It looks great.

I'd love to set up a time to go over a few questions I have before we make a decision. I'd especially like to hear more about your thoughts on revamping our company blog. Are you available for a phone conversation with my colleague Melissa Martinez and me on Thursday at 2:00?

Sincerely,

*(The email signature includes the sender's name, title, company, and contact information.)*

Michelle Marrow
Communications Manager
Little, Fields, and Young
(202) 238-2405
www.littlefieldsyoung.com

## Beginning an Email

What type of opener you use in your email will depend on what type of email you're sending.

### Formal Email

If you're writing to someone you don't know well, use a formal salutation, like this:

*Dear Ms. Whitman:*

### Informal Email

If you're writing to someone you know, such as coworkers in your office, you may use a less formal salutation, like these:

*Hi Brian,*
*Melissa,*

### Group Emails

When you have multiple people in your "To" field, it's helpful to mention them all in your opening line. This highlights for your recipients who is involved in the conversation (as they might not check the "To" field).

*Hi Linda, Kareem, Ryan, and Janet,*

Of course, if you are writing to a very large number of people, it would be unwieldy to list them all. In this case, you can simply start as follows:

*Hi everyone,*
*Hi all,*

## The Body of an Email

When you write the email message itself, keep these important points in mind:

- **Keep it short and to the point.** Email is most suitable for relatively quick messages, not for pages and pages of text.
- **Don't use long paragraphs.** If most of your message is one large block of text, recipients will find it difficult to read. Short paragraphs are easier to scan.
- **Don't use all caps.** Writing in all capital letters is considered yelling. Use normal capitalization.
- **Don't use all lowercase.** Remember basic grammar rules. While in more casual emails (or text messages) with friends, not adhering to capitalization rules may be accepted, it is highly unprofessional in the business world. Capitalize the beginning of each sentence and all proper nouns.

## Fonts and Graphics

In email, a plain and simple appearance is best. Large or unusual fonts generally appear unprofessional or even juvenile. Similarly, avoid unusual colors; plain black text on a white background is the best choice.

And because different email programs handle graphics differently, avoid using unnecessary graphics, such as a graphic in place of your signature block.

## Email Signatures

An email signature is text that appears at the end of any email messages you send. You can set up your email program to add the signature automatically to the end of your messages.

In the workplace, email signatures generally contain your name, title, company name, and contact information. How much contact information you include is up to you and the conventions of your company; some people include just a phone number, while other people include a mailing address, website address, and/or social media links.

Avoid these pitfalls in your email signature:

- **Too much text.** Keep your email signature as short as possible. Three to four lines is usually sufficient.
- **Different fonts or colors.** Using a variety of colors and fonts in your signature can look unprofessional. Keep it simple!
- **Inappropriate or unprofessional quotes.** Some people like to sign off their emails with a funny quote or other message. However, political, religious, or off-color quotes may offend others.

### The Proper Use of Emoticons

Emoticons are representations of facial expressions created by typing a sequence of characters. If you think about it, emoticons are a kind of pronoun, because they stand for something else. Emoticons were first used as a typing shortcut in the sending of informal messages and texts and are perfectly acceptable to use in personal communications. However, they do not belong in formal writing or professional correspondence.

## Emailing a Supervisor

When you're emailing a **supervisor**, pay attention to your tone, make sure to supply appropriate context, and stay brief. Your tone should be professional, upbeat, and direct. Always take care not to sound angry, defensive, or argumentative.

### Give Context

When you've been focused on a project, it's easy to forget that your manager's attention has probably been on other things. Instead of expecting your manager to remember all the details you've talked about previously, a simple reminder of context or past decisions can be very helpful. For instance, if you're checking in with your boss about a project that you've discussed in the past, assume that she's probably not as focused on it as you are and say something like, "As a reminder, here's where we are on the schedule, and this is what we talked about last month."

**Don't:** *I talked to Philip and he's on board.*
**Do:** *As you suggested when we met last week, I talked with Philip Johnson and he's willing to host the event.*

**Don't:** *Sally Kurtz will be out of the country in June.*
**Do:** *I checked with Sally Kurtz to see if she'd be willing to attend the June board meeting, as Melissa suggested in the last staff meeting, but she's going to be out of the country for all of June.*

## Stay Brief

Your supervisor is probably busy, so don't get bogged down in a lot of detail. Be concise and get to the point quickly.

**Don't:** *I've been running the numbers for those t-shirts we sold at concert venues last summer (the ones Karen designed). I've been having trouble figuring out exactly what to compare them against, but I've finally realized that we sold a similar line two years ago. I asked Jane to dig out those numbers, and I was able to compare the two. It looks like last summer's line did really well. Look at the spreadsheet I attached and you'll see how they each did.*
**Do:** *Last summer's T-shirt line outsold our similar line from two years ago by 23%. I'm attaching a chart that compares the results for each.*

# Emailing a Subordinate

When you're emailing a **subordinate**, pay attention to your tone and make sure to be clear about action items and deadlines. Remember that those you supervise might be especially sensitive to any hints of negativity from you. Take an extra few seconds to read over your email to ensure that your tone can't be misinterpreted.

### Be Clear about Action Items

If you're asking your reader to do something—whether it's working on a particular project or staying late the next day—make sure that that is clearly spelled out in your email. If you don't say it directly, the message might be lost.

> **Don't:** *I'm attaching last year's results, which will be a good benchmark to measure this year's numbers against.*
> **Do:** *Please compare our current results with last year's, which you can find in the attached spreadsheet, and let me know how this year's numbers stack up.*

### Be Clear about Deadlines

If you're assigning a piece of work, be sure to include clear direction on when it must be completed by. If there's no deadline, it's fine to say something like, "This is medium priority and ideally would be finished in the next few weeks."

# Common Mistakes and How to Avoid Them

Perhaps more than any other form of business writing, email has the potential for mistakes. Let's take a look at some of the most common email mistakes and how to avoid them.

## Tone

When you speak to someone face to face, you can hear his or her tone directly. You can tell if the person sounds upset or angry or calm. When you write an email, your recipient won't hear your tone of voice and has to rely solely on the words you write. If you don't pick your words carefully, this can lead to miscommunications. You might think that you're simply being direct, but your recipient might think you sound curt or abrasive. Or, you might think that you're making a funny joke and end up inadvertently offending your recipient.

Being aware of the potential for tone to be misinterpreted in email can help you avoid these miscommunications. You can also try reading a message out loud before you send it, to see if it sounds differently when spoken out loud than it did in your head.

And importantly, if your message is complicated or sensitive, consider talking in person or over the phone instead. Email is a useful tool, but it's not always the right choice for every message!

### Avoid Anger

**Don't:** *Why in the world didn't you tell me Samuel called? How hard would that have been?*
**Do:** *Do you know why I wasn't alerted when Samuel called?*

### Avoid Sarcasm

**Don't:** *I'm sure no one noticed that we were the only team that missed this crucial deadline today.*
**Do:** *I'm concerned that we were the only team to miss today's deadline.*

### Avoid Abrasiveness

**Don't:** *This report is unreadable.*
**Do:** *Let's talk in person about this report.*

### Sending Too Soon

Email is useful because it's so quick—you hit "send" and your recipient has your message just seconds later. But the instant nature of email can also pose pitfalls: you might accidentally send your message before you're finished writing it, or you might send it without a crucial piece of information included.

To avoid this, always read over your message carefully after you write it. Another precaution is to fill in the "To" field last. If you haven't filled out the "To" field, the message can't be sent!

### Not Reviewing All Messages Before Replying

If you open your email program and find 15 new messages, read them all before you start replying. Otherwise, you might miss important information that could change your response; one of those later messages might be a follow-up with different instructions or a note from a coworker that he or she has already handled the matter. If you respond before you've finished reading all your new messages, you might end up causing errors or confusion, or just wasting time.

### Forwarding Sensitive Emails without Permission

It's easy to forward an email with the click of a button, but before you forward a message, pause and ask yourself: Is there anything private or sensitive in the message?

If an email was intended for your eyes only, you violate the sender's trust by forwarding it to others. If you're unsure if it's okay to forward a particular email, check with the sender for permission first.

### Misusing Company Email

Your workplace email account is owned by your employer. Because the email account is their property, your employer is permitted to read anything you write or receive on company email, and many companies do monitor workplace email accounts. Be careful not to use your workplace email account for private emails. If you wouldn't want your boss to read it, don't send it with your company email!

Your company probably has a policy on workplace email and Internet use. Make sure that you read it and understand how you may and may not use your company email account.

# 7 Memos

**M**emos are generally used for internal communication within an organization. They're used to convey information about anything from a procedure change to a proposal for a new product line to a concern about a performance problem—and just about anything else you can think of, too.

## Memos versus Emails

In deciding whether to write a memo or simply send an email, it's important to know what the norms are in your workplace. Some offices use email for nearly everything, while others prefer the formality of a memo in some situations. Pay attention to how your workplace does things and adhere to those norms.

Additionally, memos are useful if you need a hard-copy record of an action or decision. Some companies also like the formality of a memo when making important announcements or policy changes.

# Formatting

When done correctly, formatting a memo is simple and straightforward.

Memos have two sections: the heading and the body.

### The Heading

The heading section identifies the recipients of the memo, the sender, the date the memo was sent, and the subject of the memo. It's usually formatted like this:

**TO:** All department managers
**FROM:** Katie Whitman
**DATE:** November 1, 2015
**SUBJECT:** Deadline for department budget proposals

### The Body

This is the discussion section of the memo. Open with the most important information, followed by any additional information readers might need to know.

Memos typically do not end with closings such as "Sincerely" or "Best regards" and do not include signature lines.

Here's an example of what a memo might look like.

### Sample Memo

**TO:** All staff
**FROM:** Carter Smith
**DATE:** October 15, 2015

*(The subject should be specific enough to communicate the purpose of the memo, e.g., "Reminder about accrued vacation days," not simply "Reminder.")*

**SUBJECT:** Reminder about accrued vacation days

*(The memo gets to the point right away, clearly stating the information it is intended to deliver.)*

As we approach the end of the year, please remember Acme's policy that vacation days accrued in 2015 must be used by December 31, 2015. Any unused vacation days will not roll over into 2016, so use them now if you don't want to lose them!

Because we typically receive many requests for time off around the holidays, be sure to submit your requests for holiday time off to your manager now, in order to have the best chance of the time off being approved.

*(The memo clearly states the next steps that readers should take.)*

If you have any questions about your accrued vacation balance, please check with Patty in HR.

# Writing an Effective Memo

When you're writing a memo, it's important to pay attention to your tone and language and present information clearly. Let's take a look at how to do that, as well as how to avoid some common mistakes.

## Tone

Workplace writing used to be stiff and formal, but norms now embrace a more conversational style—as long as you remain professional. You don't need to be stiff or overly formal in a memo. After all, you're addressing your coworkers, so a more conversational tone is fine.

Do keep emotion out of your memo, however. Remember that this document will be around for a long time, and no matter how difficult the topic, your tone should be positive or neutral (never negative) and respectful.

### Be Conversational, Not Stiff

**Don't:** *We would appreciate your notification to our company of whether or not you intend to remain an active customer.*

**Do:** *We'd love to keep you as an active customer. Would you let me know if you'd like to renew for another year?*

### Keep Emotion Out of It

**Don't:** *I'm so frustrated that I haven't yet heard back about the error in my paycheck. Is this how you treat loyal employees?*

**Do:** *I know that you're busy, but it's been a week since I reported the error in my paycheck. Could you let me know when it's likely to be resolved by?*

### Keep a Positive Tone

**Don't:** *Because you assembled the parts wrong, the machine is now broken.*

**Do:** *The machine won't work correctly if the parts are assembled out of order.*

## Presenting Information Clearly

To make your memo as clear as possible, don't bury your main message! State clearly up front what the purpose of the memo is and what recipients need to do with it—whether they need to simply read the information or take an action, such as attend a meeting, follow a new policy, or address a problem.

Read your memo over from the perspective of someone who isn't familiar with the information within it. Is the message clear rather than vague? Are there unanswered questions? Is it clear what the recipient should do next, if anything?

Don't let mistakes in your memo make it less effective. Let's take a look at some of the most common mistakes people make when writing memos and how to avoid them.

### Writing Too Much

While you might have quite a bit of information about the topic you're writing about, it probably doesn't all belong in the memo. Ask yourself what your recipients need to know, and focus on that. Don't get bogged down in unnecessary details.

### Writing Too Little

The flip side of knowing a lot about what you're writing about is that it's easy to forget that others don't have the same background and context that you do. Make sure that you give enough information that your recipients will understand your key messages. This might mean giving some brief background or an explanation of your reasoning.

### Not Making Next Steps Clear

If you want your readers to take a next step, such as changing the way they submit expense reports or attending a meeting on a different date than was originally scheduled, make sure that that's very clear in your memo. You might even bold that part of the memo so that it can't be missed!

### Not Proofreading

Grammatical or spelling errors can make you appear sloppy or unprofessional and can dilute the impact of your memo's message. Always proofread a memo or have a grammatically inclined colleague read it over for you before you send it out.

# 8 Meetings and Presentations

**H**aving an effective meeting agenda can be the difference between running a useful meeting and running a meeting that your attendees can't wait to leave. This chapter will show you how to prepare and document an effective meeting.

## Setting a Meeting Agenda

A meeting agenda provides a map for the meeting to follow and makes it clear to all attendees what will be discussed and what outcomes you're hoping to reach. Agendas keep a meeting on track and ensure that you cover everything that you need to cover, without getting sidetracked by non-essential issues. Have you ever attended a meeting without an agenda? If so, you've seen how agenda-less meetings often get off track, go on longer than planned, and end without clear decisions or action items. By contrast, meetings with agendas stay focused and productive. Attendees are all on the same page about what they're there to accomplish.

By informing people ahead of time what topics will be covered, and being as specific as possible, an agenda lets people know what to expect and why their presence is needed. Most people are also more enthusiastic about attending meetings where the agenda spells out a defined list of topics to be covered and a clear time limit for each; this lets them know that they're not risking spending their whole afternoon in a discussion that veers off course or that might not be relevant to them.

## Key Elements of an Agenda

An effective meeting agenda is based around knowing your objectives for the meeting, ensuring that each agenda item relates back to those objectives, assigning a leader and time limit for each topic, and building in some time at the end for anything unexpected that may arise.

A meeting agenda should include the following:

- Topics to be discussed
- The presenter for each topic
- The amount of time allotted for each topic

## Know Your Objectives

A good agenda starts with getting clarity about exactly what you want the meeting to accomplish. For instance, you might want to brainstorm ideas on a particular topic, discuss how to meet a challenge with a client, share important updates, or make a decision about how to move forward with a project. Once you figure out your objectives, translate them each into an item on the agenda. Try to keep the agenda focused and resist adding in items that don't relate to your goals.

**Examples of Focused Agenda Items**

- *Update on the Smithers Account*
- *Ideas for Year-End Party*
- *Status of Summer Intern Recruitment*
- *Potential Budget Cutbacks*

**TIP**

Keep in mind that if the purpose of the meeting is solely to share information and won't involve any discussion, a memo or email might be better suited to that purpose.

Once you've prepared your agenda, send it to the meeting attendees at least a full day, but preferably more, before the meeting. This will allow them to review the agenda items and prepare in advance with questions and ideas. If you don't circulate the agenda until the meeting itself, people won't have a chance to prepare and won't know what to expect.

## Assign a Discussion Leader

By assigning a discussion leader for each topic, attendees will understand who is responsible for keeping each section of the meeting on track. Be sure to alert your designated leaders about their responsibilities before the meeting time! They might not read the agenda carefully (although of course they should) and get an unpleasant surprise come meeting day.

Discussion leaders should present information and throw out questions for discussion. They can also summarize any decisions and next steps that the group comes up with.

In addition to assigning a discussion leader for each topic, note how much time is allotted to each topic. This will help the group stay on track and know when it's time to move on.

**Examples**
- *Status of Summer Intern Recruitment (Lynn, 15 minutes)*
- *Ideas for Year-End Party (Ricardo, 10 minutes)*

### Assign a Notetaker

Along with a discussion leader, it's always a good idea to designate someone to take notes. It should be someone with excellent listening comprehension and, ideally, who doesn't have a significant role in presenting information, so they can focus on recording key ideas and action items that meeting attendees contribute. After the meeting, the notetaker will be responsible for consolidating his or her notes into a summary that will be circulated among attendees and anyone else the information is pertinent to.

### Leave Time at the End

In a perfect world, every meeting would follow the agenda precisely. In the real world, topics often take longer than predicted and unanticipated questions or concerns arise that need to be discussed. It's a good idea to leave some time at the end of your meeting as a buffer for topics that went on slightly longer than expected or to address any outstanding questions or concerns.

### Sample Meeting Agendas

Look at these two samples of meeting agendas. The first shows what not to do, and the second shows what an effective meeting agenda might look like.

### *What Not to Do*

*(The header is vague about the purpose of the meeting and the date. "Tuesday" could be this week, next week, or even further in the future!)*

**Meeting Agenda**
**Date:** Tuesday

*(The topics on the agenda are vague and unfocused.)*

1. Updates on project
2. New business

*(No one has been assigned to lead each topic, and there's no indication of how long will be spent on each.)*

3. Questions
4. New projects

### What to Do

*(The header notes the date and time of the meeting.)*

**Meeting Agenda**
**Publications Planning Meeting**
**Date:** May 24, 2015, 3:30–4:30

*(The agenda lists the topics to be covered and the discussion leader and time allotted for each.)*

1. Status of summer membership guide (Marjory, 15 minutes)
2. Plans for Susan's maternity leave (Pilar, 10 minutes)
3. Update on clean water policy brief (Marjory, 10 minutes)
4. New projects (Eduardo, 15 minutes)

*(The agenda allows a small amount of time at the end as a buffer or for questions or concerns that may arise.)*

5. Other business (10 minutes)

## Meeting Summaries

After a meeting, it's good practice to write a summary of the meeting and send it to all participants and any other stakeholders.

Without a written meeting summary, it's easy for participants to forget what key decisions were made and what next steps were agreed to. A summary provides a written record that you and your colleagues can check back with if there's any confusion or uncertainty later about details, like who is responsible for what moving forward, relevant deadlines, and other action items. Otherwise, you may spend extra time trying to remember these important details, or even having to meet about the same topics all over again!

A meeting summary doesn't need to be complicated. There's no one format for meeting summaries that you must use. However, whatever format you choose should include the following:

- Date of the meeting
- Names of the people in attendance
- A bulleted list of topics discussed
- A 1–2 sentence summary of decisions made or actions agreed upon for each topic discussed
- Next steps and the person responsible for each topic, with any associated deadlines
- Any items deferred for a future meeting

If you'd like, you also can provide a summary of any areas of agreement and disagreement that aren't captured in the items above.

The purpose of a meeting summary is not to provide a transcript of what was said at the meeting. Rather, its purpose is to capture the most important points: the topics that were discussed, the decisions that were made, and any commitments or action items that should be followed through upon. You don't need to get into "Jane said X" or "Ricardo said Y."

### Sample Meeting Summaries

Here's an example of what both an ineffective and an effective meeting summary might look like.

## What Not to Do

*(The header doesn't note the date of the meeting or who was present.)*

### Meeting Summary
### Publications Planning Meeting

---

*(The summary notes that topics were discussed but in several cases fails to note what conclusions were drawn or recommendations were made.)*

- We talked about the summer membership guide.

*(There's no need to report who said what; the summary should focus on key points and conclusions.)*

- We talked about the plan for when Susan is on maternity leave. Marjory said it would be good for the group to vet the candidates who will fill in for her. Pilar agreed.

- The clean water policy brief is scheduled to be issued next month. Eduardo said that he thinks it will be ready on time, but Melinda disagrees. Pilar agrees with Melinda that we should be concerned. Ben didn't have an opinion.

*(Topics are listed without resolution or next steps.)*

- We talked about updating the corporate style guide.

## What to Do

*(The header notes the date of the meeting and those present.)*

**Meeting Summary**
**Publications Planning Meeting**
**Date:** May 24, 2015
**Present:** Marjory Carlson, Eduardo Lopez, Melinda Burns,
Ben Stoltz, Pilar Modart

---

### Discussed:

- The launch of the summer membership guide is on track. Eduardo still needs to sign off.

- With Susan preparing for maternity leave, Pilar is interviewing graphic designers to fill in for fall and winter projects.

- Melinda is concerned about progress on the clean water policy brief scheduled to be issued next month.

*(Topics deferred to the next meeting are noted.)*

- Several people have suggested updating our corporate style guide. We'll revisit this at the next meeting.

### Action Items:

*(Action items each have a clear owner and, where relevant, deadline.)*

- Pilar will forward the portfolios of the graphic designer finalists to the group by the end of the week.

- Melinda will ask Susan for an updated schedule for the policy brief and make sure we're going to hit our target publication date.

# Presentations

Workplace presentations come in all shapes and sizes—whether you're preparing a quick pitch for a meeting or getting ready to roll out company products before a crowd of stockholders, it's an opportunity for you to impress your employers and boost your reputation among your colleagues. For some people, speaking in front of a group of any size is the stuff of nightmares. For others, it's a chance to perform and show off their oratorical skills. Whichever end of the spectrum you find yourself closer to, this section provides you tools to make a great impression and express yourself successfully.

## *Public Speaking*

Your public presence is a combination of posture, volume, confidence, and conveying important information. If you find public speaking stressful, the best thing you can do for yourself is practice, practice, practice. Find something to read aloud—a speech by a famous orator, your favorite short story, even your shopping list—and stand in front of a mirror. You can also practice by recording yourself on video.

Take a deep breath, make eye contact with a spot on the wall just about the head height of your audience, and speak slowly and clearly. Enunciate deliberately, but try to maintain a natural rhythm. Do you speed up when you're nervous? How's your pitch? Higher than usual? Lower than usual? Too loud? Too quiet? Do you clear your throat or say "um" frequently? Rehearse your remarks until they are fluid and confident—having a polished delivery gives you authority and professionalism.

As you watch yourself in the mirror—or when you review the video afterwards—look for distracting or self-conscious gestures. Do you talk with your hands? It may make for lively conversation but, taken to extremes, may make you hard to watch! Perhaps you'll be seated at a table or standing behind a podium. Plan ahead and know if you'll have a place to put your hands, a water glass to contend with, or any other props to be aware of.

As you prepare for a specific public speaking gig, read your remarks out loud as you draft them—plenty of professional prose looks great on paper but sounds tortured when spoken. Look for unwieldy alliteration, unnecessary polysyllabic words that may trip you up when you're in the spotlight, dangling modifiers, run-on sentences, and tangled clauses.

## PowerPoint and Other Visual Aids

When you're giving a presentation, a program like PowerPoint can be a powerful way to enhance your talk by helping you convey your points and ideas visually. However, using PowerPoint effectively takes thought and preparation—a disorganized or confusing PowerPoint show can detract from your presentation.

### Planning Content

When working with PowerPoint, people often make the mistake of planning their content as they work within the program. But it's far more effective to plan what you want to say first and then determine what slides will most effectively support your points.

Before you begin, ask yourself what the purpose of your presentation is. Are you educating your audience on a particular topic? Trying to persuade them of a viewpoint? What do you want them to do because of your presentation—leave with more information, take a particular action, or something else?

### Designing Slides

While your slides can provide visual interest and help you augment your points, always remember that they're not the main part of your talk. Resist getting carried away with a large number of graphics, complicated charts, or design elements. The most important function of your slides is to communicate clearly and directly, not to show off your design skills. If you find yourself putting more energy into creating beautiful slides than into the content of your presentation itself, that's a signal that you might be focusing your energies in the wrong area.

Because the most important function of your slides is to convey your points clearly, don't clutter them up with too many colors, fonts, backgrounds, or art. Instead, keep plenty of white space and avoid logos or other graphics that don't contribute to the slide's core message. A simple design theme will provide a clean canvas so that the focus is on the idea you're displaying—whether it's a picture, graphic, or short amount of text.

To ensure that your slides are readable, even by people in the back of the room, pay attention to the fonts, font sizes, and colors you choose. Generally, fonts should not be smaller than 18-point, with 30-point or slightly larger being preferable. Choose easily readable and professional fonts. Times New Roman, Arial, Helvetica, and Verdana are generally appropriate choices for business presentations.

Dark text on a light background is easiest to read. However, if your company uses a template with a dark background, make sure that your text is white or a very light color so that it's readable. In that case, you might also want to increase the font size to assist with readability.

### Bells and Whistles

It can be tempting to use PowerPoint's animation features, like flashing text, fades, and other visual tricks. But too much animation can be distracting, so limit yourself to a few subtle effects. And be consistent: don't use a fade on one slide, flashing text on the next, a dissolve on the one after that, and so forth. Pick one or two effects so that they blend smoothly into your presentation without taking over the show.

### One Idea per Slide

Your audience will read each slide as soon as it's displayed. When you draft the presentation you'll be giving alongside your slideshow, make sure what you have to say isn't redundant. Don't just read the slide—expand upon it, augment it, take the opportunity for anecdotes or quick asides. The slide should just be a jumping off point for what you want your audience to consider.

Don't feel that you must have a slide to support every point of your presentation. Use slides only when they truly help reinforce or explain a concept. In fact, when you're not showing a slide, you can insert a plain white or black slide into your slide deck to keep the focus on your talk. If the next several points you plan to make are displayed, the audience will "read ahead" rather than focus on what you're saying as you say it. By ensuring that each slide contains only one point, you control the flow of information and keep your audience focused where you want them.

If a slide has too much text, your audience may lose focus, so use text sparingly. Instead of writing out entire paragraphs or blocks of text, use bulleted key points. Or try having no text at all, supporting your points with a graphic or chart instead.

## REMEMBER

The slides should support the presentation, not be the entire the presentation.

# Section 4: Grammar Skills

**N**othing is more important when presenting yourself as a professional than having good grammar—in both your speech and in your writing. Studying the following chapters will give you a much-improved grasp on how grammar works and why having good grammar is so important in your daily work life.

# Parts of Speech

**Y**ou need good grammar if you're going to communicate successfully—both orally and in written form. This book assumes that you have studied grammar previously and that you are an efficient communicator orally but that you might need reminding about some of the parts of speech and how they work together to form complete and effective sentences. This chapter reviews nouns, adjectives, verbs, adverbs, and pronouns.

## Nouns

Every sentence must include, at the very least, a noun and a verb; sometimes these are referred to as the subject and the predicate. They're easy to spot. The **noun** is the person, place, or thing doing the action in the sentence. Nouns can be **common nouns**, such as *boy*, *girl*, *dog*, *cat*, or they can be **proper nouns**, which describe a specific person, place, or thing.

| COMMON NOUNS | PROPER NOUNS |
| --- | --- |
| school | Harvard University |
| president | Thomas Jefferson |
| company | Tricity Planning |
| city | New York City |
| web browser | Google Chrome |

Be careful to follow the rules of capitalization. Being accurate about these rules can often make the difference between clarity and confusion in a sentence. Note the difference here:

John visited the White House.
John visited the white house.

The White House, when capitalized, clarifies that the writer is referring to the home of the president. Without capitalization, the writer can be describing any house that is painted white.

Common nouns are usually not capitalized, except when they are the first word in a sentence. Proper nouns are always capitalized, except when companies (or persons) have made a point of distinguishing themselves by violating the rules. For example, a famous American poet spelled his name e.e. cummings, and eBay and iPod are familiar words in our culture today.

## Practice 1: Correcting Noun Spellings

Find and correct the noun spelling errors in the following sentences.

**1.** Bluebird enterprises is relocating its headquarters to New york city.

**2.** In 1934, the american animation studio walt disney created the character Donald duck.

**3.** Thousands of nervous High School Students across america compete to become students at a prestigious University named princeton.

**4.** The small herd of buffalos in San francisco's golden gate park is a popular tourist Attraction.

**5.** How many millions of people tune in to nbc Nightly news each Day?

# Adjectives

**Adjectives** are words that describe or modify nouns or pronouns. They add information by describing people, places, or things in a sentence. These words add spice to our writing.

   **Descriptive adjectives** are the type most often associated with adjectives. Their purpose is to qualify the properties or behavior of nouns or pronouns. In the following examples, the descriptive adjective is italicized and the noun or pronoun being modified is underlined:

> The *impressive* <u>candidate</u> got the job.
> His *effective* <u>writing</u> makes a lasting impression on clients.
> Please process the *important* <u>data</u> first.

In most cases, the adjective comes immediately before the noun or pronoun it is modifying. However, the adjective is sometimes used in the predicate form. In these instances, it is found *after* the subject of the sentence. Here are some examples of descriptive adjectives in predicate form:

The <u>conference</u> was *long*.
My <u>superior</u> is *understanding*.
All the <u>computers</u> were *broken*.

## Practice 2: Identifying Adjectives

Underline the adjectives in each sentence.

1. Please check the mailroom for any important deliveries.
2. Here's a new proposal for increasing profits over the coming months.
3. I spoke with Jane about my concern over her lagging sales figures.
4. The information you provided about my order is helpful.
5. The company is launching its spring line next week.

## Verbs

**Verbs** are the words that describe the action in a sentence or that define the relationship between two things. When a verb is doing the action in a sentence, it is called the **predicate**. Verbs also define the time of the action: the present, the past, or the future.

Often verbs are accompanied by helping verbs that serve to define further the time or nature of the action.

In the following sentences, the helping verb is italicized and the verb being helped is underlined.

The accounts *were* <u>dropped</u> after two years of inactivity.
The market *is* <u>panicking</u> after the interest rate hikes.
The customers for their product *are* <u>swelling</u> in numbers.
The new employee *has* <u>arrived</u> late for the last time.

The most common helping verbs are the following:

| | |
|---|---|
| can | could |
| do | did |
| has | had |
| have | may |
| is | are |
| might | must |
| shall | should |
| was | were |
| will | would |

All verbs have four principal parts from which all other forms are derived. These four forms are **past**, **present**, **past participle**, and **present participle**. For most verbs, the past and past participle are formed by adding -*ed* to the end of the present form. Similarly, the present participle is created by adding -*ing* to the end of the present form.

| PRESENT | PAST | PAST PARTICIPLE | PRESENT PARTICIPLE |
|---|---|---|---|
| borrow | borrowed | borrowed | borrowing |
| gain | gained | gained | gaining |
| measure | measured | measured | measuring |
| ski | skied | skied | skiing |
| track | tracked | tracked | tracking |

Some verbs, however, have irregular forms when converted to the past, past participle, or present participle forms.

| PRESENT | PAST | PAST PARTICIPLE | PRESENT PARTICIPLE |
|---------|------|-----------------|--------------------|
| do | did | done | doing |
| get | got | got | getting |
| go | went | gone | going |
| see | saw | seen | seeing |
| say | said | said | saying |

Since verbs are the most complex part of speech, they have many rules. The most important consideration when using verbs is tense. Tense gives the verb a reference of time: *past*, *present*, or *future*. It also describes what has happened or what is going to happen.

The **past** tense is derived from the past part of the verb—no helping verbs are used in the past tense. Be sure *not* to use the past participle form of the verb when expressing something in the past.

> **Incorrect:** I *gone* to the store.
> I *done* what was necessary.
> I *seen* what you did.
> **Correct:** I *went* to the store.
> I *did* what was necessary.
> I *saw* what you did.

The **present** and **future** tenses are derived from the present part of the verb. Using the present form of the verb in the present tense is straightforward. If you want to express a verb in the future tense, add *will* or *shall* before the present form of the verb.

> **Present Tense:**
> They *meet* all deadlines on time.
> Marketing *designs* the product catalog.
> Operations *produces* 10,000 units per day.

**Future Tense:**
They *will meet* all deadlines on time.
Marketing *shall design* the product catalog.
Operations *will produce* 10,000 units per day.

# Practice 3:
## Identifying Verbs and Their Tenses

In the following sentences, identify present- and future-tense verbs (and their helpers) by circling them and identify past-tense verbs by underlining them. (Be careful: sometimes verbs can act like nouns.)

1.  John typed frantically as his coworkers passed his desk on their way to the emergency meeting that will begin at noon.

2.  I laughed uproariously when I realized how nervous I had been about doing well on the marketing presentation.

3.  More than two dozen species of animals peacefully inhabit the wildlife reserve.

4.  Trudging wearily through a driving snow to work every day is a common event in some parts of the Midwest.

5.  Prince, whose original name was Prince Rogers Nelson, famously began his musical career during junior high school with a small band called Grand Central.

# Adverbs

**Adverbs** are descriptive words just like adjectives. However, instead of describing nouns or pronouns, adverbs modify verbs, clauses, adjectives, and even other adverbs. Most adverbs are easily identified because the majority of them end with the suffix *-ly*. In fact, many adjectives can be converted to adverbs simply by adding *-ly*:

| | | | | | |
|---|---|---|---|---|---|
| angry | angrily | most | mostly | slow | slowly |
| glad | gladly | near | nearly | smart | smartly |
| late | lately | quick | quickly | terrible | terribly |
| loud | loudly | quiet | quietly | vast | vastly |

However, some words end in *-ly* but are adjectives (not adverbs), such as:

| | | | |
|---|---|---|---|
| costly | daily | early | lively |
| lonely | monthly | neighborly | orderly |
| timely | weekly | worldly | yearly |

In addition to these modifiers, there are two special types of adverbs: **conjunctive** and **interrogative**.

**Conjunctive** adverbs join thoughts and phrases:

| | | | |
|---|---|---|---|
| however | nevertheless | then | therefore |

Funding is important in business; *however,* there's more to it than that.

The last round of fundraising was unsuccessful; *nevertheless,* they must continue.

If the company can find the funding, *then* it can proceed with the expansion.

The funding did not come through; *therefore,* the expansion is delayed indefinitely.

**Interrogative** adverbs are *how, what, where, when,* and *why*. They ask questions that modify verbs, clauses, adjectives, and adverbs and usually appear at the beginning of a sentence.

> *When* are the labor talks?
> *Where* is the marketing department?
> *Who* is in charge of overseeing the company's hiring practices?

When using adverbs, it is best to place them as near as possible to the word or clause it is modifying. Here the adverb is italicized and the word it is modifying is underlined.

**Poor form:**
The supply department <u>ran out</u> of spare parts *nearly*.
We <u>must remember</u> the customers *also*.
They <u>remember</u> what they're supposed to do *scarcely*.
**Good form:**
The supply department *nearly* <u>ran out</u> of spare parts.
We *also* <u>must remember</u> the customers.
They *scarcely* <u>remember</u> what they're supposed to do.

# Practice 4: Identifying Adverbs

Reread the five sentences from Practice 3, in which you identified verb forms, and circle the adverbs.

1. John typed frantically as his coworkers passed his desk on their way to the emergency meeting that will begin at noon.

2. I laughed uproariously when I realized how nervous I had been about doing well on the marketing presentation.

**3.** More than two dozen species of animals peacefully inhabit the wildlife reserve.

**4.** Trudging wearily through a driving snow to work every day is a common event in some parts of the Midwest.

**5.** Prince, whose original name was Prince Rogers Nelson, famously began his musical career during junior high school with a small band called Grand Central.

# Noun-Verb Agreement

In every sentence you write, the noun and the verb must agree in number. This means that a singular noun must be paired with a singular verb, and a plural noun requires a plural verb.

## Exceptions to the Rule

Compound subjects usually take a plural verb, but occasionally a compound subject expresses a single idea and can take a singular verb. Here are some examples:

War and peace is a common subject for debate in political circles.
Love and marriage is the theme of many advertising campaigns.

Compound subjects joined by *or* and *nor* usually agree with the noun closest to that word. The use of *either/or* and *neither/nor* dictates that each of the nouns is to be treated individually as the single subject of the sentence and, therefore, a singular verb is correct. Here are some examples:

Either a tote bag or a t-shirt would make a good promotional gift. (singular verb for singular *t-shirt*)

Either Mike or his coworkers are going to attend the seminar. (plural verb for plural *coworkers*)

## Practice 5: Identifying Correct Verb-Noun Agreement

Choose the correct verb in the following sentences.

1. Colored text and graphics (*make, makes*) the report more exciting and colorful.

2. The actors auditioning for a place in the show (*is, are*) waiting in the lobby of the theatre.

3. Would-be managers often (*take, takes*) years to acquire leadership skills.

4. The charts in the report (*doesn't, don't*) convey accurate information about our sales last quarter.

5. Either a college degree or relevant prior work experience (*is, are*) required to be considered for the position.

## Pronouns

The proper use of pronouns is a bit complicated, but once you think about them, you'll realize that you use them every day, all the time, without hesitation. The trick is knowing when to use which one of the many pronouns available in English. A **pronoun** is a word used in place of a noun or of another pronoun. The word that the pronoun refers to is called its **antecedent**.

There are several categories of pronouns. The ones we use most often, and that you need to pay special attention to, are personal pronouns, possessive pronouns, reflexive and intensive pronouns, and interrogative pronouns. In all these different types, the function of the pronoun is about the same: it replaces another word or group of words.

The grammatical function the pronoun serves in a sentence is called its case, which defines whether the pronoun is being used as the subject of the sentence, as the object of another word, or in a possessive or reflexive form.

## Personal and Possessive Prounouns

Personal pronouns are the pronouns that you probably use most often. Here's a chart that categorizes their correct forms:

| SINGULAR PERSONAL PRONOUNS | | | |
|---|---|---|---|
| | SUBJECTIVE | OBJECTIVE | POSSESSIVE |
| first person | I | me | my, mine |
| second person | you | you | your, yours |
| third person | he, she, it | him, her, it | his, her, hers, its |

| PLURAL PERSONAL PRONOUNS | | | |
|---|---|---|---|
| | SUBJECTIVE | OBJECTIVE | POSSESSIVE |
| first person | we | us | our, ours |
| second person | you | you | your, yours |
| third person | they | them | their, theirs |

## The Correct Use of Personal Pronouns

There are some basic guidelines for using personal pronouns. The **subjective** form is used if the pronoun is the subject of the verb. For example:

> *I* directed the marketing strategy segment of the meeting at last night's conference.

*You* were the person responsible for the department's turn-around.

*He* wrote the report that was sent to the customer.

*They* decided not to expand operations at this time.

When using a personal pronoun with a linking verb (any form of the verb *to be*: *am, is, are, was, were*), the pronoun that follows *to be* should be in the subjective form. The examples below show the verb underlined and the pronoun in italics.

That <u>is</u> something *I* would say.

Who <u>are</u> *we* to judge?

The contracts <u>were</u> a responsibility *they* should have handled.

**↪ TIP**

> A good way to check for accuracy with linking verb sentences is to turn the sentence upside down and see if it sounds right. For example, *He is the top chef at the restaurant* sounds right; and *Him is the top chef at the restaurant* does not sound right.

There are three instances that require the use of the **objective** form of pronouns. The first is when the pronoun is the direct or indirect object of the verb.

My supervisor gave *us* the day off.

The gold watch was a present for *you*.

Patience is not one of *her* qualities.

He told *them* the account was overdue.

The second is if the pronoun is the subject or object of an infinitive. Here the infinitive is underlined and the pronoun is italicized.

The chairman requested *me* <u>to attend</u> the conference.

The finance department is the place for *you* <u>to start</u> a career.

There was no other place for *them* <u>to visit</u>.
The data was difficult for *him* <u>to comprehend</u>.

The third rule for using the objective form is if the pronoun is an object of a preposition. In these examples, the preposition is under-lined and the pronoun is italicized.

If the client likes the ideas, then go <u>for</u> *it*.
Suddenly, the solution came <u>to</u> *him*.
The plaintiff is in agreement <u>with</u> *us*.

The **possessive** form of pronouns is used to indicate possession.

*Their* thoughts were much clearer in the morning.
The lecture was *his* last of the evening.
*Our* outing proved to be fruitful in many ways.

## Practice 6: Choosing the Correct Personal Pronoun

In the following sentences, choose the correct personal pronouns. Then identify them as subjective, objective, or possessive.

1. This is an example where (*he, him, his*) should have spoken up.

2. The report did not differ much from (*you, yours*).

3. After the moderator introduced the speakers, (*he, his, him*) asked (*their, them, they*) some compelling questions.

4. We launched (*us, our, ours*) new line before the competitors launched (*them, theirs, their*)

5. (*You, Your*) told (*I, me, mine*) that your computer was faster than (*my, I, mine*).

> ⤷ **TIP**
>
> Using the right personal pronoun is one of the hardest lessons for students and adults alike. Study the chart on page 180 carefully until you are sure you know the difference between subjective and objective pronouns. Then, whether you are speaking or writing, try always to consider whether you are using a pronoun as the main subject of the sentence or clause (the person or thing doing the action) or if you are using the pronoun to describe the person or thing having something done or said to them.

## Special Reminder: The Linking Verb Rule

When a pronoun functions as the object of a linking verb (any form of the verb *to be*, for example, *is, am, are, was, were, been, can be, will be, should be*), you must use the subjective form of the pronoun.

## Reflexive and Intensive Pronouns

You use reflexive and intensive pronouns all the time, even if you don't remember their category names. They are easily identified because they all end in *-self* or *-selves*. **Reflexive pronouns** refer to the subject of the sentence and direct the action of the sentence back to the subject. Reflexive pronouns are essential to the sentence's meaning.

> They talked among *themselves.*
> He appointed *himself* to the committee.

**Intensive pronouns** emphasize another pronoun or noun in the sentence.

> The employees *themselves* wrote their handbook.
> I *myself* have always been a morning person.

> **⤷ TIP**
>
> If you delete the reflexive pronoun from the sentence, it doesn't make grammatical sense. Intensive pronouns, on the other hand, are not essential to the sentence's meaning.

## Demonstrative Pronouns

**Demonstrative pronouns** (*this*, *that*, *these*, *those*) are fairly easy to use. They demonstrate what you are talking about; they point out a noun. Here are some examples:

> *This* is the building's blueprint.
> *Those* receipts have not been submitted.

> **⤷ TIP**
>
> A common mistake that many writers and speakers make is to double up and add the words *here* or *there*. For example, an inexpert writer might make mistakes like these:
>
> This *here* project is driving me crazy.
> That *there* order is the largest we've ever had.
>
> Be careful not to insert extra words.

## The That-Which Confusion

Use the pronoun *that* when the clause that follows it is essential to your sentence. Use the pronoun *which* (with a comma in front of it) when the clause it introduces can be deleted from the sentence without destroying its meaning. For example:

> The memo *that* went out last week is incorrect.
> The mailroom, *which* was once on the second floor, is now on the first floor.

# Interrogative Pronouns:
# Is It *Who* or *Whom*?

There are several interrogative pronouns, and they're easy to spot. (Remember that the word *interrogative* is related to *interrogation*, a word you probably know from detective shows on TV.) **Interrogative pronouns** ask *who* and *whom*.

> *Who* is always used as a subject. *It* replaces *he* or *she*.
> *Who* is attending the reception?
> The best candidate for the position is *who*? (Linking verb takes a subject.)

*Whom* is always used as an object. *It* replaces *him, her,* or *them*.

> With *whom* are you going to the reception?
> You gave *whom* the position?

# Practice 7: Using Correct Pronouns

Choose the correct pronouns in the following sentences.

1. To become a good writer, you need to determine (*what, which*) is your ultimate goal.

2. To (*who, whom*) should I direct my questions about the proposal?

3. Surely you will want to thank (*your, you're*) coworkers for all the support they gave you.

4. My first attempts at grant writing made (*their, they're*) way into the trash bin.

5. Just between you and (*I, me*), I'm disappointed by this month's sales figures.

# Answers

## *Practice 1: Correcting Noun Spellings*

1. Bluebird Enterprises is relocating its headquarters to New York City.
2. In 1934, the American animation studio Walt Disney created the character Donald Duck.
3. Thousands of nervous high school students across America compete to become students at a prestigious university named Princeton.
4. The small herd of buffalos in San Francisco's Golden Gate Park is a popular tourist attraction.
5. How many millions of people tune in to NBC Nightly News each day?

## *Practice 2: Identifying Adjectives*

1. Please check the mailroom for any <u>important</u> deliveries.
2. Here's a <u>new</u> proposal for increasing profits over the <u>coming</u> months.
3. I spoke with Jane about my concern over her <u>lagging</u> sales figures.
4. The information you provided about my order is <u>helpful</u>.
5. The company is launching its <u>spring</u> line <u>next</u> week.

## *Practice 3: Identifying Verbs and Their Tenses*

Present and future tenses are circled; past tenses are underlined.

1. John <u>typed</u> frantically as his coworkers <u>passed</u> his desk on their way to the emergency meeting that (will begin) at noon.
2. I <u>laughed</u> uproariously when I <u>realized</u> how nervous I <u>had been</u> about doing well on the marketing presentation.
3. More than two dozen species of animals peacefully (inhabit) the wildlife reserve.
4. Trudging wearily through a driving snow to work every day (is) a common event in some parts of the Midwest.

**5.** Prince, whose original name <u>was</u> Prince Rogers Nelson, famously <u>began</u> his musical career during junior high school with a small band called Grand Central.

## Practice 4: Identifying Adverbs
Adverbs are circled.
  **1.** John typed (frantically) as his coworkers passed his desk on their way to the emergency meeting that will begin at noon.
  **2.** I laughed (uproariously) when I realized how nervous I had been about doing well on the marketing presentation.
  **3.** More than two dozen species of animals (peacefully) inhabit the wildlife reserve.
  **4.** Trudging (wearily) through a driving snow to work (every day) is a common event in some parts of the Midwest.
  **5.** Prince, whose original name was Prince Rogers Nelson, (famously) began his musical career during junior high school with a small band called Grand Central.

## Practice 5: Identifying Correct Verb-Noun Agreement
  **1. a.** make
  **2. b.** are
  **3. b.** take
  **4. b.** don't
  **5. b.** are

## Practice 6: Choosing the Correct Personal Pronoun
  **1.** he (subjective pronoun)
  **2.** yours (possessive pronoun)
  **3.** he, them (objective pronoun)
  **4.** our (possessive pronoun), theirs (possessive pronoun)
  **5.** You (subjective pronoun), me (objective pronoun), mine (possessive pronoun)

## *Practice 7: Using Correct Pronouns*

1. what
2. whom
3. your
4. their
5. me

# 10 Sentence Structure

This chapter focuses on the various types of sentences and pays particular attention to common sentence errors, such as sentence fragments and comma splices.

Sentences are made up of words put together to communicate ideas. Every grammatically correct sentence must have a **subject** (the noun doing the action) and a **predicate** (the verb describing the action). Once words are combined to communicate ideas, they are called **clauses**. Clauses can be either independent or dependent. **Independent clauses** express a complete idea (*I interviewed candidates.*) **Dependent** (or subordinate) **clauses** do not express a complete idea but contribute to (or modify) the independent clause in a sentence (I interviewed candidates *when the hiring freeze was over.*)

# Three Kinds of Sentences

There are three kinds of sentences: simple, compound, and complex. Look at the following examples to see how they differ from each other.

1. **Simple sentence:** The receptionist loves to greet visitors.
     Simple sentences contain one independent clause that expresses a complete thought.
2. **Compound sentence:** The receptionist loves to greet visitors, and he always offers them coffee or tea.
     Compound sentences contain two (or more) independent clauses and no dependent clauses.
3. **Complex sentence:** Because the receptionist is gregarious, the office gets a lot of visitors.
     Complex sentences contain one independent clause and one or more dependent clauses.

When a sentence combines compound and complex sentences, containing two or more independent clauses as well as one or more dependent clause, it is called a **compound-complex sentence**.

Because the receptionist is gregarious, he loves to greet visitors, and he always offers them coffee or tea.

> **⤳ TIP**
>
> Here are a few sentence structure rules:
>
> - Simple sentences are not necessarily short, but they contain only one independent clause.
>
> - In compound sentences, the two (or more) independent clauses must be related in thought.
>
> - In complex sentences, the dependent clause clarifies the relationship between ideas. Often, these dependent clauses start with words like *because*, *when*, *who*, or *where*.

# Practice 1: Identifying Sentence Structure

For each sentence, identify its structure type. Underline independent clauses once. If there are dependent clauses in the sentences, underline them twice.

**1.** Sacramento is the capital of California, so its local economy focuses on keeping political and business interests actively involved with one another.

**2.** Kim fired the employee when his absences became excessive.

**3.** Please stop at the security desk to obtain a visitor's pass.

**4.** When the hiring freeze was over, Chet called Matt, and Jeff yelled, "You are hired!" in the background.

**5.** When deciding whether or not to send a letter or an email, the most important factor is what the norms are in your workplace or industry.

# Sentence Fragments

A common error is to write sentence fragments. **Sentence fragments** are sentences that lack one or more of their essential elements—a subject or, more commonly, a predicate (the verb).

They typically occur when you are following up on a thought but close the thought too soon, leaving the rest of your idea hanging out as a fragment. You can correct the fragment by either joining it to an independent clause or by rephrasing it to make it an independent clause on its own.

Following are several examples of sentence fragments and ways to correct them. The fragments are underlined.

> **Incorrect:** We went to the conference in Los Angeles. After the meeting in San Diego.
>
> **Correct:** We went to the conference in Los Angeles after the meeting in San Diego.
>
> **Incorrect:** Deborah had just met Mr. Brizgy. The new surgery center chief surgeon from Europe.
>
> **Correct:** Deborah had just met Mr. Brizgy, the new surgery center chief surgeon from Europe.
>
> **Incorrect:** Mike worked all day Saturday. Finishing the annual budget right before the board meeting that evening.
>
> **Correct:** Mike worked all day Saturday, finishing the annual budget right before the board meeting that evening.

**Incorrect:** Jack came to the meeting without his briefcase. <u>Which was so typical of him.</u>

**Correct:** Jack came to the meeting without his briefcase. This act was so typical of him.

### How to Avoid Writing Sentence Fragments

Read every sentence you've written aloud very slowly. If you've written a fragment, you'll hear your voice stop in midair at the end of the sentence. This is because in our natural rhythm of speech, we drop our voices at the end of a sentence, which is usually when the idea of the sentence is complete. Usually when you read a fragment aloud, your voice at the end will sound as if it is dangling off the edge of a cliff.

After reading every sentence aloud, go back through your writing and check each and every sentence to make sure that it falls into one of the three sentence structure categories. Remember, every sentence must have at least one subject and one predicate.

# Practice 2:
# Identifying Sentence Fragments

Read the following sentences aloud. Which are complete sentences, and which are sentence fragments?

1. Because I am trying to improve.
2. Using big words to impress the reader.
3. Talking is not so different from writing.
4. Writing can be difficult.
5. Adopted a long-term approach.

> **TIP**
>
> You will sometimes notice that writers use fragments for effect. (This book sometimes uses fragments, for example.) Fragments are allowed only when they are used carefully, and for dramatic effect or to emphasize a point. As you read, note carefully the use of fragments; analyze why the writer has chosen to ignore the strict rules of grammatical sentence structures. In your own writing, you'll be much safer if you obey the rules.

## Run-On Sentences

Another common error is run-on sentences. **Run-on sentences** occur when you join sentences without putting a punctuation mark in between or when you simply join them by putting a comma between them. They can be corrected by using a semicolon, using a comma and a conjunction, or by making two complete sentences, each closed with a period.

> **Run-on:** Adopting a long-term approach is the most sensible solution, the company cannot lose sight of this.

Notice that *Adopting a long-term approach is the most sensible solution* and *the company cannot lose sight of this* are each able to stand alone as independent clauses. They each make sense. If you join such complete thoughts with a simple comma, then you have created a run-on, and also the impression that you don't take care with your writing.

> **Correct:** Adopting a long-term approach is the most sensible solution; the company cannot lose sight of this. (*You can use a semicolon to correct the run-on.*)

Adopting a long-term approach is the most sensible solution, and the company cannot lose sight of this. (*You can use a comma and a conjunction to correct the run-on.*)

Adopting a long-term approach is the most sensible solution. The company cannot lose sight of this. (*You can make two complete sentences to correct the run-on.*)

You can check your writing for run-ons in the same way you check for sentence fragments: by reading aloud and by making sure that the sentence doesn't attempt to say too much, all in one breath.

# Practice 3:
# Identifying Run-on Sentences

Read the following sentences aloud. Which are correct sentences, and which are run-ons?

1. Marketing designs the product catalog it meets all of its deadlines on time.

2. Computers are very popular gifts during the holidays, they often go on sale.

3. If you do a lot of careful planning, both this week and next, I'm certain that the reception will be a success.

4. The president is the only person who can approve the request, she is the type of person who takes her time before making a decision.

5. The news outlets report that the market is panicking after the interest rate hikes.

## ⤳ TIP

Here are a few hints on how to avoid common sentence structure errors:

1. Check each sentence you write, carefully, for complete thoughts and for the appropriate subject-predicate pairs.

2. Read each of your sentences aloud to see if your voice drops naturally at the end of the sentence. If it doesn't, you've probably written a fragment.

3. Slow down. Rushing to get your work finished is a common trap, and very often the rush will produce sentence fragments and/or run-ons.

# Answers

## Practice 1: Identifying Sentence Structure

1. Compound
2. Complex
3. Simple
4. Compound-complex
5. Complex

## Practice 2: Identifying Sentence Fragments

1. Fragment
2. Fragment
3. Complete
4. Complete
5. Fragment

## Practice 3: Identifying Run-On Sentences

1. Run-on. Correct: Marketing designs the product catalog; it meets all of its deadlines on time.
2. Run-on. Correct: Computers are very popular gifts during the holidays, when they often go on sale.
3. Correct
4. Run-on. Correct: The president is the only person who can approve the request. She is the type of person who takes her time before making a decision.
5. Correct

# 11 Punctuation

**P**unctuation allows you to convey certain tones and inflections on paper that might otherwise be lost or misinterpreted. In essence, punctuation allows you to send a message without using your voice or your body language. It tells your reader whether you are excited, happy, angry, or just writing a matter-of-fact statement. If you punctuate effectively, your writing can seem almost as though you are right there in person, which is the desired effect of most workplace writing.

Restructuring the punctuation in a sentence can alter its meaning as easily as changing the actual words in the sentence. Using proper punctuation gives a sentence emphasis where it is needed and also separates longer sentences into more easily defined and understood segments. There are dozens of different punctuation marks in the English language, but those covered in this section are the ones most often used in workplace writing today.

# Commas

The **comma** is perhaps the single detail that causes more difficulties and gets writers into more trouble than any other element in writing. Using them correctly, however, just may convince your readers that you care enough about them to be careful with your writing. So pay attention here; you can learn to use commas correctly with some thought and a little practice.

## *The Proper Use of Commas*

1. Use commas to separate two sentences joined by a coordinating conjunction (*and, but, for, or, nor, yet, so*).

   Winston Mays won the company award, *and* he later went on to become CEO.

   Erika fixed the copier, *but* it broke again that same afternoon.

   Either you honor the contract, *or* the company will be forced to take action.

   I have written the entire contract, *but* the attorneys must approve it.

2. Use commas after introductory words or phrases.

   *With the exception of yesterday,* the process has run fairly smoothly.

   *No matter what,* I'll always look back on this experience fondly.

   *As much as she wanted to,* she couldn't let go of the issue.

   Some introductory elements are as simple as words of emphasis:

   *No,* I don't think that is wise.

   *Recently,* Marcy began to think differently about the project.

Clauses that start with *although* are also set off by commas:

*Although it seemed unlikely,* we remained hopeful.

The radio broadcast was excellent, *although it was a little difficult to hear over the static.*

3. Use commas to insert an interrupting element in a sentence.

There are still details, *as you may recall,* that need clarifying.

The test results will come back, *I believe,* a week from Monday.

4. Use commas to separate words and word groups in a series of three or more.

*Brian, Robin, and Annelise* met with the auditors to review the balance sheet.

The board of directors will *interview the staff, compile the information, and then present it to the stockholders.*

Giancarlo enjoyed solving *pressing, puzzling, technological* issues at the company.

First *two, then three, then four* rabbits appeared on the lawn.

5. Use commas to separate two adjectives when the word *and* could be inserted between them.

Gladys thought it was a *successful, positive* interview.

Gladys thought it was a successful *and* positive interview.

Do not use a comma if *and* cannot be used to separate the adjectives:

His resume showed his extensive educational background in research. (You could not say "*extensive and educational* background in research.")

6. Use commas to surround the name or title of a person directly addressed.

> Will you, *Hilde,* take on the directorship of the landscape committee?

> Yes, *Doctor Gershweir,* I will.

7. Use commas to separate the day of the month from the year and after the year.

> *December 7, 1941,* is a day that will always be remembered in American history.

If any part of the date is left out, omit the comma:

> *December 1941* is an infamous month in American history.

8. Use commas to surround degrees or titles used with names.

> *Leslie Worden, PhD,* got a job in the city she preferred.

> *David Pfaff, Vice President of Marketing,* would be proud to see the work done in his name.

9. Use a comma to separate the city from the state.

> Working in *Sacramento, California* has been a wonderful experience.

10. Use a comma to introduce quotations. Remember to put the comma inside all quotation marks.

> *"Hiring him was a huge mistake,"* Dr. Hannah Rose stated.

> *"Why,"* the boss asked Stewart, *"are you always the last to leave the lab?"*

## Beware the Comma Splice

**Comma splice** is the term used to describe the incorrect use of a comma; it is called a splice because the most common error is to splice (or slice) a sentence, dividing two independent clauses with only a comma. Beware the comma splice. It is the most common comma error, and it results from a writer's uncertainty, ignorance about comma rules, or just plain negligence.

## ⮑ TIP

When in doubt about a comma, leave it out. You have a better chance of conveying meaning without a comma than you do with sticking one in arbitrarily and thereby splicing the sentence unnecessarily.

# Practice 1: Using Commas Correctly

Insert commas in the appropriate places in the following sentences.

**1.** A long river the Mississippi can be said to divide the United States into two parts west and east.

**2.** When you are traveling west from Philadelphia Pennsylvania you arrive in Chicago long before you arrive in Salt Lake City.

**3.** "Seeing the country by car" said the tour guide "is really the best way to learn what being an American is all about."

**4.** Getting to a scheduled airline flight these days can be very difficult due to the requirement that you take off your shoes and jacket throw away your water bottle and show your ticket before you enter the gate area.

**5.** On the other hand there is no mode of travel that is faster easier simpler and more modern than air flight.

# Periods and Other End Marks

Use **periods** at the ends of sentences that neither exclaim nor ask a question but simply make a statement.

> I think the company newspaper should come out only twice a month.

Use **question marks** to end a direct question.

> What time does your meeting begin?

Reserve the **exclamation point** for use in sentences that express very strong feelings.

> If Lenore hadn't called it to my attention, I would have missed my plane!

The **ellipsis mark** is three spaced periods used when omitting something from a quotation. Do not use them when using your own words in place of a dash. There are several rules that cover different circumstances that occur depending on where the omitted piece falls in the quotation.

1. If you omit words from the middle of a quotation, mark the omission by using three spaced periods.

   > "Mr. Jones, *standing rigidly in front of the hostile crowd,* replied bitterly to the question posed by the reporter."
   > "Mr. Jones . . . replied bitterly to the question posed by the reporter."

2. If you omit the end of the quotation, simply add a fourth period.

   > Barry Brown ended the presentation with the ringing words, "This will mark the beginning of the end. . . ."

Barry Brown was actually heard to say, "This will mark the beginning of the end *for corporate America*."

3. If you omit words that follow a completed sentence, add the ellipsis mark to the period already there.

Cathy Dafoe began her presentation by stating, "Sadly, what you are about to hear from me will simply sustain your current fears. . . . "

Cathy actually said, "Sadly, what you are about to hear from me will simply sustain your current fears. *Our corporate profits have plummeted at an unprecedented rate, and we are facing bankruptcy.*"

---

### ⇨ TIP

Beware! You should be very stingy with your exclamation marks. They can quickly lose their power if you use them too often. And a sure sign of a weak writer is one who uses exclamation points to convey meaning or emotion instead of using the words themselves to express the ideas.

---

## Practice 2: Using End Marks

Choose the proper end mark to use in each of the following sentences.

1. Are you buying the building as an investment

2. I heard that they have been working on the government project for months

3. The company forfeited its chance to submit a proposal

**4.** For which degrees has she studied

**5.** The attachment you sent contained a computer virus

## Quotation Marks

**Quotation marks** give credit to borrowed words that you use in your own text and words that are used for special emphasis.

> The senior partner was a *"thorn in my side."*
> After that presentation, I finally understand what is meant by *"seeing is believing."*

Also use quotations when reporting a direct statement. When commas and periods come next to quotation marks, they always appear *before* the quotation marks.

> Megan Dickinson declared, "You haven't seen the last of me!"
> "You haven't seen the last of me!" declared Megan Dickinson.
> "You," declared Megan Dickinson, "haven't seen the last of me!"

Don't use quotation marks in an indirect statement:

> Megan Dickinson told our group that we hadn't seen the last of her.

'Single quotation' marks are used when you are quoting something inside of an already existing quote.

> Dan specifically advised all employees to "watch the stock prices go rocketing upward today, as Alan Greenspan has said there will be yet another *'significant interest rate drop.'*"

**TIP**

Commas and periods always go inside closing quotation marks.

# Colons and Semicolons

Use a **colon** to introduce a list when you **don't** use the words *for example* or *such as.*

> *The firm ordered its usual supplies:* magnets, flasks, and beakers.
> *Our invoice needs to show the following:* bills of lading, dock fees, and telephone charges.

Do not use a colon after a verb or a preposition.

> **Incorrect:** Our usual supplies *are:* magnets, flasks, and beakers.
> **Incorrect:** We will serve our customers *with:* diligence, speed, and respect.

Also use a colon to follow the greeting in a business letter.

> Dear Sir:
> Dear General Worden:

The **semicolon** is generally used where you could also use a period. It is best used as a kind of weak period, a separator of contrasts. Its strength comes in the joining of two sentences to form a compound sentence without the help of a connective word. For the semicolon to be appropriate, the sentences it joins must be closely related in meaning. If they are not, simply use a period.

> Let's take care of that Wednesday; we'll have more information by then.
> The problem is not with accounting; it is with management.
> The soft-drink company did well for its first ten years in operation; however, later it incurred debt that led to its eventual bankruptcy.

Semicolons can also be used instead of commas to separate items in a series when one or more items have commas of their own.

> Adrian asked Harris, from Reginald, Inc.; Cecilia, from Klaus & Co.; and Jordan, from Fowley Products.

Unlike commas, exclamation marks, and periods—which fall *inside* the quotation marks—colons and semicolons fall *outside* quotation marks.

> She said she thought my work "went above and beyond"; I hope this leads to a raise in salary.

## Hyphens and Dashes

**Hyphens** and **dashes** are used to connect or set off specific words in your sentences.

Use a hyphen to join compound words.

> The most *well-known* speaker is the CEO from Jacob Drivers, Inc.
> It is unwise to *self-diagnose* your health ailments.

His *self-discipline* slipped as he responded angrily to the unfounded accusations.

The *commander-in-chief* of the air force and his family had many fond memories of the countries where they had lived.

Use a hyphen in compound numbers from twenty-one to ninety-nine and in fractions that are used as adjectives.

A total of *thirty-nine* employees will be at the picnic.

*Two-quarters* cup of water is all that the recipe calls for. (adjective)

*One third* of the work is completed. (noun)

The **em dash** essentially does the same job as parentheses, but in a lighter-handed manner. Em dashes indicate an interruption in thought. Remember to place two consecutive em dash marks together for correct punctuation form.

Michael Jordan—basketball legend, golfer, baseball star—regularly made the cover of news magazines.

The em dash may also be used to define a word if the context is not sufficient for the reader to gain the meaning of the word.

The barracoon—a place where slaves were held for sale in Africa—was burned to the ground.

A single em dash may emphasize an added comment.

Cade could be the CEO of the company—provided he finishes his advanced degree.

# Apostrophes

**Apostrophes** are used to indicate ownership and to form contractions.

A general rule with apostrophes is to add *'s* to form the singular possessive.

> The *quarterback's* pass was intercepted.
> The *lawyer's* brief was masterfully prepared.
> *Chris's* client signed the contract.

Note that the rule applies even when the singular noun ends in *s*, such as *Chris*.

A few plurals not ending in *s* also form the possessive by adding *'s*.

> The *children's* clothing line will be launched in April.
> *Women's* rights were achieved by the active work of many.

Possessive plural nouns already ending in *s* need only the apostrophe added.

> The *drivers'* complaints were sent to headquarters.
> Five *carpenters'* toolboxes were left at the building site.

Indefinite pronouns show ownership by the simple addition of *'s*.

> *Everyone's* hard work paid off.
> *Somebody's* calling to inquire about the rental listing.

Possessive pronouns never have apostrophes, even though some may end in *s*.

> *Our* family business was founded by my grandfather.
> *His* performance record is erratic.

Show possession in the last word when using names of organizations and businesses, in hyphenated words, and in joint ownership.

> *Ben and Caryn's* company logo was a gavel and a textbook.
> I encased my *great-grandmother's* locket in a special box frame.
> The meeting of the *Organization of American States'* members took place in February.

Apostrophes may also be used to form contractions by taking the place of a missing letter or number. These contractions—shortened forms of common expressions—are acceptable both in spoken English and in informal writing. Do not use contractions in highly formal written presentations:

> *We're* (we are) ready to launch a new line of cosmetics.
> *She's* (she is) going to be on the next flight.

The following table can help you remember the differences between some common possessive pronouns and contractions.

| POSSESSIVE PRONOUN | CONTRACTION |
| --- | --- |
| whose (whose friend) | who's (who is) |
| your (your friend) | you're (you are) |
| their (their friend) | they're (they are) |
| its (its head) | it's (it is) |

# Practice 3: Using Other Punctuation Marks Correctly

Add the correct punctuation to the following sentences.

1. The advertisement spoke perfectly for the organization it displayed intelligence wit and tradition.

2. The three book series was a best seller in the summer of 1998.

3. He wanted to go whether or not he was invited the meeting was too important to miss.

4. The conferences luncheon was challenging to organize on her own she should have asked for assistance.

5. Im very honored said Sandra who was the twenty second artist to be selected.

# Answers

## *Practice 1: Using Commas Correctly*

1. A long river, the Mississippi can be said to divide the United States into two parts, west and east.
2. When you are traveling west from Philadelphia, Pennsylvania, you arrive in Chicago long before you arrive in Salt Lake City.
3. "Seeing the country by car," said the tour guide, "is really the best way to learn what being an American is all about."
4. Getting to a scheduled airline flight these days can be very difficult due to the requirement that you take off your shoes and jacket, throw away your water bottle, and show your ticket before you enter the gate area.
5. On the other hand, there is no mode of travel that is faster, easier, simpler, and more modern than air flight.

## *Practice 2: Using End Marks*

1. Question mark
2. Period
3. Period
4. Question mark
5. Exclamation point

## *Practice 3: Using Other Punctuation Marks Correctly*

1. The advertisement spoke perfectly for the organization; it displayed intelligence, wit, and tradition. *or* The advertisement spoke perfectly for the organization—it displayed intelligence, wit, and tradition.
2. The three-book series was a best-seller in the summer of 1998.

**3.** He wanted to go, whether or not he was invited; the meeting was too important to miss. *or* He wanted to go, whether or not he was invited—the meeting was too important to miss.

**4.** The conference's luncheon was challenging to organize on her own; she should have asked for assistance.

**5.** "I'm very honored," said Sandra, who was the twenty-second artist to be selected.

# Section 5:
# The Writing Process

This section includes specific techniques for planning and executing your workplace writing successfully. You'll learn strategies for generating writing, how to organize your writing once you've completed a draft, big-picture ways to think of structuring your paragraphs, introductions, and conclusions, and approaches to revising your work. Half the achievement of becoming a strong writer is knowing how to edit.

The tools you'll learn in this section are adaptable to any format or genre, from a long-term project proposal to a quick memo.

# 12 Prewriting

Often the hardest part of the writing process is deciding what to say. That blank page, or that flickering empty screen, can be intimidating. How to begin?

This chapter introduces you to some techniques that can help you figure out how to get started. The frustration at the beginning of the process can often be minimized if you use some low-stakes exercises to get you over the early writing hurdles.

## Brainstorming

### *Group Brainstorming*

**Group brainstorming** is an activity in which several people work together to come up with a solution to a problem. For an allotted time period (usually 10 to 15 minutes), members of the group throw out ideas quickly, never stopping to evaluate or criticize each other's ideas. One member may write the ideas on a whiteboard or record them quickly on a piece of paper or computer. At the end of the timed brainstorming session, the group reads over its ideas and comes up with a plan for moving forward.

## Personal Brainstorming

You can also brainstorm on your own to come up with ideas for your writing project. Ask yourself a lot of questions; any of them might spark an idea that will help you get started with your writing. Write down your questions and answers without stopping to edit them.

Here are some examples of questions you might ask yourself:

- What is the most important thing I want my audience to understand?
- What is exciting about the subject I'm writing about?
- What do I really want to accomplish with my writing?
- Why am I having trouble getting started writing?

You can easily answer all of these questions with a little thought. As soon as you find yourself hesitating at one of the questions, stay with it for a while. You may have struck upon the right way to begin writing.

## Tips for Brainstorming Effectively

- Establish a time limit for yourself. Depending on the amount of time you have to write (an hour, a day, a week, etc.), your brainstorming session might be as short as 15 minutes or as long as an hour one day and another hour a day later, once you've had time for your ideas to simmer overnight.
- Write down ideas, without editing or polishing them, as quickly as you can. Jot down whatever comes to you—individual words, phrases, questions—and don't worry about their making sense or appearing in order.
- Once your time is up, take a deep breath and try to clear your brain.
- Now look over the ideas you've brainstormed and evaluate them. Cross out the ideas that strike you as unworkable;

underline the ideas and/or words that strike a chord in your brain. Add to the brainstorming list if related or additional ideas come to you.

- Somewhere within your jottings you have undoubtedly written something that can be used to begin your writing.

# Mapping Your Subject

In the constant search to find ways to make their writing easier, writers use various techniques to help organize their thoughts and plan their work. One of the simplest devices used for planning is called a **cluster diagram**, or a **concept map**.

Concept maps can be very useful brainstorming tools. If you tend to think in pictures, you may find that jotting down your ideas during the planning stage in map form is a helpful way both to get your ideas down on paper and to visualize the relationships between various ideas. Here is a sample concept map created by a marketing professional who is exploring the relationship between sports and popular culture.

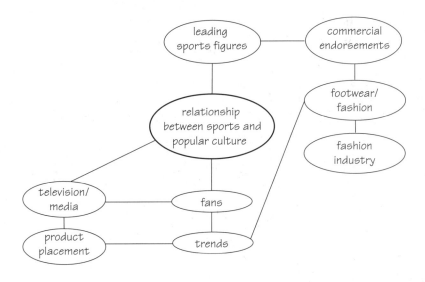

There is no right or wrong way to create a concept map, and it is important that you do not censor yourself when you're drawing it. Write down your ideas in any order, and draw circles (or ovals or stars) around each idea to keep it separate from other ideas. Then sit back and consider them. See if you can find relationships among the ideas, and if you do, connect them with lines or arrows. You may want to cross out some of your ideas that don't contribute to the logic or map of the topic that has emerged during the drawing of the concept map.

Below you'll see a concept map drawn by a writer doing the preplanning for a report about environmental issues that her company could address in its new campaign. Note that she has been careful to try to create the map in a very orderly fashion, with ideas radiating in a prioritized manner—big ideas lead down to smaller ideas.

You may not think in such an orderly way, and your maps might not look so tidy, which is perfectly all right. What's important is to get lots of ideas down on paper so that you can reorganize your ideas into a different order once you sit down to write the draft of your text.

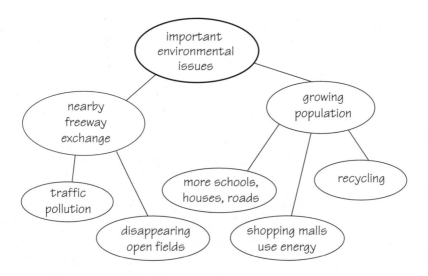

A similar tool that many writers find useful is **a mind map**. To create a mind map, the writer starts from a central idea, drawn usually in a circle in the center of the map, and related ideas are generated in circles radiating out from the central idea. Writers who prefer mind maps to concept maps emphasize that the mind map allows them to think randomly, without having to create big ideas that generate smaller ideas below them. Using a mind map, the writer visualizes all of his or her ideas as being of equal weight; subsequent planning will then, of course, require that ideas be reorganized into generalizations and specifics. Here is an example of the mind map that the writer who planned to write about environmental issues might have created.

## Practice 1:
## Creating a Mind Map

Create a mind map for your self-evaluation. Start with the words *my performance* in a center circle. Spend just three minutes creating ideas for this evaluation. Think through your responsibilities, strengths and weaknesses, and possible areas for improvement.

Remember, there are no right and wrong answers. This exercise will help you understand how useful mind maps can be in helping you plan any and all kinds of writing tasks.

## Practice 2: Creating a Concept Map

Now take another three minutes and draw a concept map for the topic, "What Is My Five-Year Plan?"

Remember that concept maps usually visualize ideas in a prioritized pattern or format (general ideas → specific examples), but you are not required to draw your maps in any prescribed way. This exercise will help you know which kind of map feels right to you.

Are you a mind map person or a concept map/cluster diagram person? Think about why you prefer one technique over the other. Perhaps you'll want to take these assignments to work and discuss them with your colleagues. Your employer might be delighted to have you demonstrate these strategies for your coworkers.

## Freewriting

Many writers warm up by doing practice writing sessions, called freewriting. **Freewriting** is the practice of writing continuously (usually in a timed session), without pausing to correct spelling, grammar, or sentence structure. If you get stuck and can't think of anything more to write, then you write about that. ("I am stuck and can't think of anything else to write . . . oh, wait I just realized how I feel about. . . .") Freewriting can be thought of as the written form of idle thinking, the kind of mind wandering you do when you're commuting, or waiting to fall asleep, or daydreaming during a particularly boring meeting.

During freewriting, you don't worry about staying on topic. Many find that it's easier to begin their freewriting with a specific topic or question, no matter how simple or vague, and then to let their writing take them anywhere. Once you're started writing, you let your mind (and your fingers) do the choosing. You may find yourself coming up with connections and ideas you wouldn't have come to had you been using some other planning technique to begin your writing.

Here's a sample of freewriting done by a writer preparing to write a memo about the benefits of different kinds of media in marketing planning. Note that the freewriting veers off the subject occasionally, but that the writer manages to come up with several ideas that might be reorganized into specific examples and relevant points for the finished memo.

*My goal here is to determine what types of media outreach would be most beneficial to our company, Danielle's Dog Spa and Daycare, at this stage in our growth as an organization. My instinct would be to consider local newspaper ads first as these have the most direct contact with our local customers, but I can also see the benefits to partnering with our suppliers and distributors for some kind of promotion, or providing our clients with flyers or discounts they can pass along to their friends and fellow dog owners. I like the idea of magnets with our company logo and contact information, or of doing seasonal goodie bags as mailings—my cleaning service does that and it makes me want to recommend them very highly to everyone I know. I know that my boss is interested in raising our profile dramatically, and she wants me to consider television ads but I just don't think that we have the bandwidth to either afford that kind of expense to make a really good ad, or to handle the influx of business that might come in if we made a really effective one. I would prefer to partner with our dogwalking employees or our food suppliers to make our daycare a big neighborhood draw. However if we hope to expand in the next year, we need to move in to new markets. Last time I was in my friend Suzanne's neighborhood we went to the movies and I noticed there were billboard style ads before the commercials and trailers started—maybe that would be a good compromise and a way to cultivate a neighborhood-specific buzz about our business. We could include a map of the area we currently serve and announce we're extending our dogwalking coverage to wherever the ad is running very soon.*

## Organizing Strategies

Organizing your thoughts before writing is absolutely critical. It is possibly the most important step in the entire writing process.

When organizing your thoughts, it is essential to remember to stay focused on the big picture—be sure you are sailing in the correct ocean. Think everything through first. Don't bog yourself down in the details, or you will sail right off course into the abyss.

Commonly used organizational methods in workplace writing include the following:

- **Alphabetical:** A common way to organize information such as lists of global office locations or office supplies is by the letter in the first word. In this book, the list of commonly confused words is organized alphabetically.
- **Chronological:** Company history information, meeting minutes, and corporate calendars are usually organized by date or time. You can start with the most recent event or the earliest event.

- **Deductive method:** Used by attorneys—often referred to as *IRAC*: Issue, Rule, Application/Analysis, and Conclusion. You begin with a general issue. Then you state the rule of law, then how that law applies to your issue, and finally, what conclusions can be drawn—or, why your side should win. This method is also used for sales or promotional letters and is excellent for business proposals.
- **Inductive method:** You begin with details and examples and build up to the general issue by citing supporting evidence along the way. You might use this method if you are addressing a problem.
- **Inverted pyramid:** Used for general business correspondence (letters, memos, reports) and also for writing books. You begin with the overall layout and then emphasize key elements in order of decreasing significance. Your goal is to bring different parties to mutually pinpointed focus—to be on the same page.
- **List:** This method is a basic list of the fundamentals—using either bullets or numbers. Some examples are a list of company rules, supply needs, or future goals.
- **Order of location:** This method is used to define territories or regions—often used in marketing. A sales executive for a cellular company might write a report on cellular sales volume by region. Television advertisement marketing strategies are often drawn up using order of location.
- **Priority sequence:** Issues are listed in order of priority, starting with the most important and ending with the least important. This method is perfect for proposing a set of steps or procedures; a construction project would be drawn up this way.
- **Problem/solution:** This method is used to simply state a problem and then describe how to solve it or how it was solved. It usually ends with a synopsis of the expected or final outcome.

## *Time to Outline!*

Once you have decided which organizational method suits your purposes, you are ready to create an **outline**. A full-scale outline is necessary only when your document is longer than a few paragraphs, but it is still helpful to draw up a plan before you start writing. An outline serves as an overview of your intended subject matter and can be written with or without Roman numerals, capital letters, Arabic numerals, etc.

Following is an outline written by a senior account representative, describing his understanding of the facts after meeting with a client:

**Sample Outline**

**I. Overview**

    A. List meeting attendees

    B. Company direction

**II. Discussion of Topics**

    A. Electronic EOR Download Process

        1. Manual bill payment

        2. Info-systems go-ahead to move into production

        3. Commend all parties involved in project

    B. Claim record processing

        1. Automatic weekly update of *OUCH* system

        2. NADR system features

            a. Alleviates repetitive data entry

            b. Provides more detailed claimant information

    C. Provider file upload process

        1. Electronically upload provider demographic info

        2. Requires a PPO pricing database

        3. Complex process to be tabled pending further discussion

    D. Employer-level bill processing and reporting

        1. Allows clients to receive reports at employer level

        2. This system not currently needed—table the issue

**III. Use of the AMN in surrounding states**

    A. Provide document outlining savings to DCHO

    B. Provide DCHO with provider directories for other states

**IV. *OMNET* Leasing**

    A. DCHO will lease access to *OMNET* worker's comp network

    B. Conduct further discussions regarding potential agreement

**V. Business Objectives**

Your outline helps you set the direction of your writing. It forces you to weed out unnecessary words and stay focused on your goal. In an outline, you start with clear thinking, then define your major points, and finally rearrange them until they make sense. It also helps to list all supporting details or facts—subcategories—so that you have the substantiation you need in your final drafted writing.

# 13 Drafting

I t is a rare writer who can produce a polished, finished piece of writing in the first draft. Chances are you'll make mistakes, remember ideas later that you need to insert early on in your draft, leave out crucial points, or wander off on tangents. Think of the rough draft as a framework or a simplified structure built on the ideas you developed during your planning and outlining work. Some of the ideas from your freewriting may translate with minimal revision; others may have turned out just to be jumping off points for wherever you eventually land.

## Paragraph Structure

As you are aware, all writing projects include a series of paragraphs—the building blocks of all written work. (If you listen carefully to yourself and others, you'll realize that you actually speak in paragraphs as well. The shifts from one paragraph to another in spoken language are usually indicated with pauses, or questions, or responses from your listener.) Paragraphs are not just arbitrary breaks in your writing; they are created to perform several specific functions:

- to provide support for the main idea of the writing
- to indicate shifts in subject matter or time
- to provide rest for the reader's eyes—a chance to breathe

**TIP**

Pay attention to the length of your paragraphs. A series of very short paragraphs will feel choppy or disconnected. Extremely long paragraphs make reading through them difficult—they seem to take the reader's breath away. Used carefully, one-sentence paragraphs can make a dramatic impact, but be careful not to overdo this strategy.

## Requirements of a Good Paragraph

Every paragraph, whether it's the first or the last, must contain the following features:

1. A topic sentence that presents the main idea of the paragraph. The topic sentence does not necessarily come at the beginning of the paragraph—it sometimes appears at the end of a paragraph, as a kind of punctuation mark to the paragraph.
2. A series of additional sentences, all of which contain information that support, develop, or amplify the idea in the topic sentence. These sentences provide unity to the paragraph.
3. A smooth and logical flow. All the sentences in each paragraph should connect to each other easily and logically. The reader should not feel any bumps in the road as the paragraph moves along.

> **TIP**
>
> Check every paragraph you write to make sure that it has all three ingredients: a topic sentence, development of the topic, and logical flow throughout.

# The Introduction

Whether you're writing a memo, a research report, a business proposal, or a quick note to a coworker, you want to make a good first impression. The introduction is your chance to capture your reader's interest and set the tone for the writing that follows.

In some texts, the introduction is the first sentence of the first paragraph. If you are writing a whole book, you might include an introduction of as few as five or as many as 20 pages, depending on your subject. What's most important is to write an introduction that is in proportion to the whole piece of writing. For text of three to five pages, an introduction of anywhere from one to three paragraphs is probably appropriate.

## What a Good Introduction Should Accomplish

Your goals in writing the introduction paragraph are similar to your goals for the whole project. In general, you want to interest the reader and make a convincing argument for your point of view. Specifically though, the introduction has some particular goals. Here are goals to seek in writing an introduction to any piece of writing:

1. Grab the reader's attention.
2. State your main idea clearly and concisely.

3. Provide any necessary background information.
4. Establish an appropriate tone and level of formality.

There is no right way to write an introduction. As long as you have met these four criteria, you are more or less free to be creative and imaginative in constructing your introduction.

Do pay special attention to the fourth criterion. You need to match your tone to your subject carefully. For example, if you are writing about a very serious subject (such as sustainable development), you probably will want to write in formal language, which may still be personal but probably shouldn't be full of jokes and slang. On the other hand, if you are writing about your first day as a parent, you may adopt an informal tone that includes a good amount of humor.

## Strategies for Writing an Effective Introduction

Here are seven strategies to grab your reader's attention.

1. Begin with a shocking statement.
   A writer planning a report about global warming that focuses on polar bears might open with a shock like this:

   *In 50 years, there will be no more polar bears on the planet.*

2. Ask a startling question.

   *Are you willing to allow a polar bear to die of starvation?*

   This question combines two strategies: it provides a challenge to the reader and simultaneously shocks with its suggestion that polar bears might starve. This is a stronger opening sentence than one that asks, "Is global warming harming polar bears?" That is a perfectly legitimate opening question, but not a particularly strong one.

3. Quote an authority on your subject.

   *"In a shrinking ice environment, the ability of polar bears to find food, to reproduce, and to survive will all be*

*reduced," said Scott Schliebe, Alaskan polar bear project leader for the U.S. Fish and Wildlife Service.*

Finding a quotation strong enough to serve as your introductory statement can be difficult, but it may be worth the hunt. If you haven't found a good quotation in print, consider doing some telephone interviewing; you may find someone who will give you the kind of quotation you're looking for.

4. Describe an imaginary scenario.

   *Think of what the world would be like if there were no more polar bears, no more ice pack, no more Arctic Circle at all.*

   Be careful when you construct an imaginary scenario; you have to create a believable—if extreme—situation, or your reader will dismiss you immediately as an illogical thinker about to make a ridiculous argument.

5. Begin with an anecdote.

   *Research scientists in the Canadian Wildlife Service are reporting dramatic declines in the polar bear population. Eyewitness accounts by field workers describe the bears as growing visibly skinnier because they can't find enough food.*

   Newspaper and magazine writers frequently use this strategy to set the scene for the article that is to follow.

6. Set the scene with interesting background information.

   *Global warming may be a difficult subject for the individual to grasp, but field workers in the Canadian Wildlife Service are finding the global problem reduced to a very local level as they conduct their annual demographic count of polar bears in the western coastal area of Manitoba.*

   This opening statement introduces the general subject of global warming but quickly brings it to the local level to make the subject more easily grasped by the casual reader.

7. Adapt a familiar quotation or phrase to your subject matter.

> *To be concerned about global warming, or not: that is the important question facing every person in the world right now.*

This twist on Hamlet's famous speech about the moral choices he faces is a dramatic use of a famous quotation. The writer assumes that the reader will recognize the quotation and associate the seriousness of the problem about to be discussed in the report with the difficult choices Hamlet faces.

## Practice 1: Evaluating Introductory Sentences

For each pair of introductory sentences, choose which is stronger.

1. **a.** Our new proprietary software platform is very exciting.

   b. The new Job and Career Accelerator™ is going to completely revolutionize the way our clients conduct their job searches and get hired.

2. **a.** Social media is a ridiculous tool for a company to use.

   **b.** The controversy surrounding the use of social media in the workplace, either by individual users or for professionals developing a casual online corporate presence, is a continuing concern for marketing professionals and PR departments alike.

3. **a.** My favorite company initiative is "Free bagels day," for a very surprising reason.

   **b.** Free Bagels Day has absolutely changed my life.

# Writing a Strong Conclusion

A strong conclusion is as important as a strong introduction. In fact, you can turn the rules and strategies for introductions upside down and apply them to writing a conclusion. Just as you want your writing to start off strongly, you want it to end with an equivalent dramatic power.

Perhaps the most common mistake that writers make is to run out of steam and allow their texts to wind down slowly, like a clock losing battery power. Avoid this common writer's error and instead construct powerful conclusions that leave your audience with a good impression.

Like introductions, the lengths of conclusions vary. If you're writing a lengthy research report, your conclusion will be correspondingly long and will probably contain a summary of your findings. On the other hand, if you're writing a short memo, your conclusion will probably be proportionally shorter, and no longer than the last paragraph of your essay. Whatever its relative length, the conclusion needs to fulfill certain goals.

## Strategies for Writing a Strong Conclusion

The following strategies will help you write a powerful conclusion.

1. Restate the main idea.
   This is the most common way that writers conclude their writing, and the most easily abused technique. Simply restating the main point is useful as a reminder to the reader, but it can be a very unimaginative device. Try to figure out a way to provide some amplification or a twist that will keep the reader interested.

2. Shine some new light on the subject.
   A strong conclusion provides the reader with some new understanding of your subject. It might be helpful to

think of your conclusion as the gift that the reader will receive for making the journey with you to your concluding argument.

3. **Stay on target.**
Some writers, in their panic at the end of the writing project, stray off subject and conclude by opening up a new, somewhat related, subject for discussion. Avoid this trap. Be sure that your conclusion is an extension of the rest of the text.

4. **Get the reader involved.**
With the use of specific details, you can encourage the reader to make personal associations with your argument and feel the same emotions that you feel about your subject. Another way to get the reader involved is to challenge him or her to consider your argument directly; alternatively, be daring and challenge the reader to dispute an argument you've made very strongly.

In addition, consider the following strategies that are similar to the ones suggested in the discussion of introductions.

5. **Ask a question.**
A well-constructed text can often lead to a dramatic question at the end that challenges the reader in effect to contribute to your argument. Imagine that you are writing about the value of standardized tests. The following question might introduce your concluding paragraph:

> *Can we be sure then, at the very least, that these standardized tests are providing valuable information?*

6. **Quote an authority on your subject.**
Here's a quotation from an authority on standardized testing that could be used in a conclusion.

> *In the February 2014 issue of Science magazine, researchers Nathan R. Kuncel and Sarah A. Hezlett of the*

*University of Minnesota conclude that: "Standardized admissions tests are valid predictors of many aspects of student success across academic and applied fields."*

You don't necessarily have to use a quotation that agrees with you. Maybe a quotation from the opposition will provide a way for you to contradict a known authority and make a strong case for your side of the argument.

**7.** Provide a relevant anecdote.

Your personal experience (or someone else's) might provide a strong punch at the end of your essay.

*The experience of 150 seventh-graders at Centreville Middle School who took the standardized test in English usage is instructive: while 80% of the students were above average in their class work, only 56% passed the standardized test. Perhaps most damning of all, 53% of the students got lower grades in subsequent months. School administrators attributed this decline in study habits and class attendance to the dramatically lowered morale among the students.*

This anecdote would work best for a report that is critical of the use of standardized tests.

**8.** Offer a solution or a recommendation.

Depending on your subject matter, providing a workable and realistic solution may be a difficult challenge, but it can be powerful.

*Whether or not standardized tests will continue to be part of national policy is at this time unknowable. Nevertheless, there is little doubt that local schools need to enhance their commitment to building writing skills among their students. Without better preparation, students will be ill prepared to succeed in their future lives, much less in the taking of standardized tests.*

This example sidesteps the challenge of offering a solution or alternative to the use of standardized testing by concluding that there is a larger, more important issue at stake. This is clever writing and provides the reader with a loftier subject to contemplate.

9. Challenge the reader to action.
   A call to action can be an effective way to conclude.

   *Complaining about the use of standardized tests doesn't get anybody anywhere. These tests are here to stay. The energy that students (and their teachers) devote to criticizing the testing policies would be better spent figuring out ways to beat the tests and perform brilliantly on them. That'll show those test writers!*

10. Make a prediction.
    Find a way to guide your reader to look to the future.

    *Twenty years from now, we'll all look back on the controversy about the use of standardized tests and laugh. The real problem facing schools by then is going to be what to do with the multiple languages our students will be speaking. With the increasing presence of recent immigrants in our schools, schools are going to find that 40% of their students are not native English speakers. Printing standardized tests in many languages will be the least of our problems!*

## Practice 2: Writing Strong Conclusions

For each introductory sentence, write a brief a description of your ideas for a strong conclusion and explain which strategy you would use.

1. The new Job and Career Accelerator is going to completely revolutionize the way our clients conduct their job searches and get hired.

2. The controversy surrounding the use of social media in the workplace, either by individual users or for professionals developing a casual online corporate presence, is a continuing concern for marketing professionals and PR departments alike.

3. My favorite company initiative is "Free bagels day," for a very surprising reason.

# Answers

## *Practice 1: Evaluating Introductory Sentences*
1. b
2. b
3. a

## *Practice 2: Writing Strong Conclusions*
Answers will vary.

# 14 Revision

Once you've finished your first draft, you're ready for the essential next step—the revisions that will polish your rough draft. This chapter shows you how to evaluate what you have written and edit your document to make it the best it can be.

## Revising Individual Paragraphs

Think of each paragraph as a mini-essay, with a beginning, a middle, and an end. Take a good hard look at each paragraph to see if it has the following elements and performs the appropriate functions.

- Each paragraph should contain one controlling idea. Usually this idea appears in a topic sentence at the beginning or the end of the paragraph. All the additional sentences in the paragraph should relate to this one main idea. If you find sentences that do not relate to the paragraph's main idea, move them out!

- Each paragraph should develop its controlling idea sufficiently. The topic sentence of your paragraph, even if it comes at the end of the paragraph, requires support. If you find paragraphs of only one or two sentences, you have probably not developed the paragraph's idea in enough detail.

- Each paragraph should be directly related to the main idea of the entire text. Too often writers stray from their original outline and write paragraphs on topics that do not support the main idea. If you find a paragraph like this, cross it out!

- Each paragraph should contribute to the development of the main idea. Effective writing creates a progression of thoughts that culminate in a strong conclusion. Think of your text as a rolling snowball: it should get bigger and stronger the further along it goes. If it doesn't, you haven't organized well.

- Each paragraph follows the previous one with logical transitions. You may need only a word or two to create the transition between paragraphs, or you may need a sentence or two. Whatever you do, do not rely on trite transitions like *in summary*, or *on the other hand*, or *in conclusion*. Skilled writers can do better than that.

## Rechecking Your Introduction and Your Conclusion

Once you've analyzed and revised individual paragraphs, it's important to take a close-up look at your introduction and your conclusion to ensure that they are as strong and clear as you can make them. Don't be a pushover critic; make yourself revise until these elements are of the highest quality.

# The Six Characteristics of Good Writing

Every time you revise a writing project, check to see if your writing exhibits all six of the required characteristics of good writing.

1. well-developed ideas and content
2. good organization
3. consistent and appropriate tone and voice
4. powerful and engaging word choice
5. variety in sentence structure
6. correct grammar, spelling, and punctuation

# Proofreading Techniques

1. Do not proofread when you are tired and up against a tight deadline. You are certain to miss errors. Plan to have at least an hour's rest between your last revision and your final proofreading. Ideally, let your writing rest before you proofread and print out the final version.
2. Read your text aloud—very, very slowly. Reading silently at a normal pace is likely to allow you to miss errors. Often the sound of your voice making a verb error, or a pronoun agreement error, will alert you to a problem.
3. Read only one line at a time. Do this by printing out your writing, and then cover it with another piece of paper from the bottom of the page, leaving visible only one sentence at a time. This technique will focus your eyes more narrowly and enable you to consider sentences word by word.

4. Read backward. Publishers use this technique to proof-read the text they plan to put on book jackets. Reading backward, word by word, helps the proofreader to catch spelling errors.

5. Slow down. This is the most important strategy of all. Reading aloud in a normal voice or reading silently at a normal rate may not help you catch all errors.

6. Check for common errors. There are four common kinds of errors writers make that you should always look for.

   • **Check for Run-Ons and Fragments**

   Run-ons and sentence fragments are the two most common errors made by writers. Reading your text aloud, slowly, should help you catch any of these your eye doesn't catch on careful reading.

   • **Check for Agreement in Your Sentences**

   Pairing a singular verb with a plural noun—or a plural noun with a singular verb—is common. Here is a typical error:

   > *Jeremy, like his colleagues, work from home one day a week.*

   *Jeremy* is the subject, so the verb in the sentence should be the singular *works*.

   Also be on the lookout for incorrect pronoun use. Writers too often pair a singular pronoun with a plural noun, or a plural pronoun with a singular noun.

   > *Jeremy, like his colleagues, enjoys their flexible work schedule.*

   Here the writer has paired a plural pronoun (*their*) with the singular subject of the sentence. It is the plural word (*colleagues*) in the clause in between the noun and the verb that has caused the writer to make the error. The verb in this sentence is correct. *Jeremy* is the subject of the sentence; he alone is doing the acting.

• **Check for Misspelling of Confusing Words**

Confusing words often get missed by writers who are not proofing slowly and carefully enough. Pay particular attention to word pairs such as *your/you're, they're/their/there, affect/effect,* and *advise/advice.* Similarly, watch out for frequently confused verbs such as *lie/lay, sit/set,* and *lend/loan.* Review Chapter 4 to make sure you've got all these confusing pairs straight in your mind.

• **Check for Punctuation and Capitalization Errors**

Incorrect punctuation and capitalization are the easiest mistakes to overlook. As you're proofreading, make sure that

- every sentence begins with a capital letter
- every sentence ends with a period (or the correct end mark)
- there are no comma errors
- the first word of a complete sentence in quotation marks is capitalized
- apostrophes are used correctly with possessive nouns

# 15 A Final Review

A s you have learned throughout this book, writing well requires thoughtful planning, observance of the rules of grammar and spelling, attention to detail, and, most important of all, a commitment to thinking hard and doing it right.

This final chapter provides a list of the book's tips that you should remember every time you sit down to write. Review these tips to make sure you understand them. If you make these tips your own personal rules for writing, you're certain to write better.

### TIP 1: The Single Best Way to Improve Your Writing

The single most effective way to improve your writing doesn't involve writing at all. The secret: read! Reading even only 15 minutes a day, every day, will improve your writing.

### TIP 2: Slow Down

The most useful practice you can develop as a writer is to slow down. Proofread and edit your writing very carefully, and you're certain to catch a lot of errors in advance of submitting your work to other readers.

### TIP 3: Identify Your Audience Before You Begin Writing
The more specifically you have your reader in mind, the more focused and fluent your actual writing will be.

### TIP 4: How to Get Jumpstarted
If you're having trouble getting started, try a prewriting strategy, such as brainstorming or freewriting.

### TIP 5: Know the Rules for Sentences
- Simple sentences don't have to be short, but they must contain only one independent clause.
- In compound sentences, the two (or more) independent clauses must be related in thought.
- In complex sentences, the dependent clause clarifies the relationship between ideas. Often these dependent clauses start with words like *because, when, who,* or *while.*

### TIP 6: Know How to Avoid Common Sentence Structure Errors
- Check every sentence you write for complete thoughts and for the appropriate subject/verb pairs.
- Read each sentence aloud to see if your voice drops naturally at the end of the sentence. If it doesn't, you've probably written a fragment.
- Slow down. Rushing to get your work finished is a common trap that often produces fragments and/or run-ons.

### TIP 7: Use Punctuation Marks Correctly
- Commas and periods always go inside closing quotation marks.
- Question marks go inside or outside quotation marks, depending on your meaning.

### TIP 8: Avoid the Five Most Common Writing Errors

1. Comma splices are misplaced commas; learning to avoid them and/or correct them can lead to significant improvements in your writing.
2. In every sentence you write, the noun and the verb must agree in number.
3. Verb endings are tricky; they must be checked and used correctly.
4. Pronouns must agree in number, in person, and in function with their antecedent.
5. Misspelling frequently confused words is a common error that can easily be avoided. Rely on a dictionary, not a spellchecker, to check confusing words.

### TIP 9: Your Paragraphs Are Your Building Blocks

- Check and double-check every paragraph of your essay to make sure that each paragraph either supports or expands on your main idea.
- Create meaningful transitions between paragraphs; avoid clichéd connecting phrases such as *on the other hand*, *in conclusion*, and *in summary*.

### TIP 10: Vary Your Paragraph Lengths

- A series of very short paragraphs will feel choppy or disconnected.
- Extremely long paragraphs are difficult to read through—they seem to take the reader's breath away.
- Used carefully, one-sentence paragraphs can make a dramatic impact, but be careful not to overdo this strategy.

### TIP 11: Avoid These Bad Writing Habits

- wordiness
- repetitiveness
- clichés and slang

- using a thesaurus to find impressive words
- rushing to finish and therefore making grammatical errors

**TIP 12: Adopt the Six Characteristics of Good Writing**
1. well-developed ideas and content
2. good organization
3. consistent and appropriate tone and voice
4. powerful and engaging word choice
5. variety in sentence structure
6. correct grammar, spelling, and punctuation

# Practice 1: Reviewing the Final Review

Reading lists is difficult; everyone tends to skim. Go back and reread slowly and carefully the list of tips in this lesson. Highlight in yellow or circle in red the tips that reminded you of problems you have had in your writing.

Once you have created a list of personal problem areas, go back to the table of contents at the beginning of the book and look for the lessons that address your problems. Review those chapters.

Once you've done this review, you're ready to go on to the post-test.

# POSTTEST ▶

**N**ow that you've spent a good deal of time improving your grammar and writing skills, take this posttest to see how much you've learned. If you took the pretest at the beginning of this book, you have a good way to compare what you knew when you started with what you know now.

When you complete this test, grade yourself and then compare your score with your score on the pretest. If your score now is much higher, congratulations—you've profited noticeably from your hard work. If your score shows little improvement, perhaps you should review certain chapters. Do you notice a pattern to the types of questions you got wrong? Whatever you score on this posttest, keep this book handy and refer to it when you are unsure of a grammatical rule.

# Posttest

1. Which of the following is a sentence fragment (not a complete sentence)?
   a. The memo was distributed on Friday.
   b. Although the managers and the support staff had been called.
   c. The company was being acquired by a large corporation.
   d. Be sure to attend the meeting.

2. Which version is correctly capitalized?
   a. After we headed west on interstate 70, Paul informed us that his Ford Taurus was almost out of gas.
   b. After we headed west on Interstate 70, Paul informed us that his Ford Taurus was almost out of gas.
   c. After we headed West on Interstate 70, Paul informed us that his Ford Taurus was almost out of gas.
   d. After we headed West on interstate 70, Paul informed us that his Ford taurus was almost out of gas.

3. Which version is punctuated correctly?
   a. That building, with the copper dome is the state capitol.
   b. That building with the copper dome, is the state capitol.
   c. That building, with the copper dome, is the state capitol.
   d. That building with the copper dome is the state capitol.

4. Which version is punctuated correctly?
   a. The temperature was 80 degrees at noon; by 6:00 P.M. it had dropped to below 40.
   b. The temperature was 80 degrees at noon, by 6:00 P.M. it had dropped to below 40.
   c. The temperature was 80 degrees at noon by 6:00 P.M., it had dropped to below 40.
   d. The temperature was 80 degrees at noon by 6:00 P.M. it had dropped to below 40.

**5.** Which version is punctuated correctly?
  **a.** It was one managers' idea to offer employees a month's vacation.
  **b.** It was one manager's idea to offer employees a months vacation.
  **c.** It was one manager's idea to offer employees a month's vacation.
  **d.** It was one managers idea to offer employees a month's vacation.

**6.** Which version is punctuated correctly?
  **a.** "Watch out! yelled the police officer. There's an accident ahead."
  **b.** "Watch out!" yelled the police officer. "There's an accident ahead."
  **c.** "Watch out"! yelled the police officer. "There's an accident ahead."
  **d.** "Watch out! yelled the police officer." "There's an accident ahead."

**7.** Which version used parentheses correctly?
  **a.** Please load the presentation (which Shonda finished yesterday) onto the computer in the conference room.
  **b.** Please load (the presentation), which Shonda finished yesterday, onto the computer in the conference room.
  **c.** Please load the presentation, which Shonda finished yesterday (onto the computer in the conference room).
  **d.** Please load (the presentation which Shonda finished yesterday) onto the computer in the conference room.

**8.** Choose the subject that agrees with the verb in the following sentence.

_____ of the board members have arrived at the meeting.

   **a.** Each
   **b.** Neither
   **c.** One
   **d.** Two

**9.** Which of the following sentences is most clearly and correctly written?
   **a.** Bart told us all about the proposal he pitched while we waited for the conference call to begin.
   **b.** In the conference room, Bart told us about the proposal he pitched while we waited for the call to begin.
   **c.** As we waited for the conference call to begin, Bart told us about the proposal he pitched.
   **d.** As we waited for the call to begin, Bart told us about the proposal he pitched while waiting.

**10.** Which version is in the active voice?
   **a.** The president of the P.T.A. requested donations for the new auditorium.
   **b.** For the new auditorium, donations had been requested by the P.T.A. president.
   **c.** Donations for the new auditorium were requested by the president of the P.T.A.
   **d.** Donations were requested by the P.T.A. president for the new auditorium.

**11.** Which version has a consistent point of view?
    **a.** Last Sunday, we went canoeing on the Platte River. You could see bald eagles high in the trees above us.
    **b.** While we were canoeing last Sunday on the Platte River, high in the trees above us, you could see bald eagles.
    **c.** We went canoeing last Sunday on the Platte River, and high in the trees above us, we could see bald eagles.
    **d.** High in the trees above, the bald eagles were looking down at you, as we canoed on the Platte River last Sunday.

**12.** Which version uses punctuation correctly?
    **a.** Help! Do you know where I can find a website developer on short notice.
    **b.** Help! Do you know where I can find a website developer on short notice?
    **c.** Help? Do you know where I can find a website developer on short notice!
    **d.** Help: Do you know where I can find a website developer on short notice?

**13.** Which of the underlined words in the following sentence should be capitalized?

The <u>professor</u> has been teaching <u>history</u> at the <u>university</u> of California since last <u>fall</u>.

    **a.** professor
    **b.** history
    **c.** university
    **d.** fall

For questions 14 and 15, choose the correct verb form.

**14.** When she was asked which employee should be promoted, Ms. Garcia _____ Caroline Martin.
  **a.** has chosen
  **b.** choosed
  **c.** choose
  **d.** chose

**15.** The snow _____ to fall late yesterday afternoon.
  **a.** began
  **b.** begun
  **c.** had began
  **d.** begins

**16.** Which version is most clearly and correctly written?
  **a.** Jeff told Nathan that his computer battery was dead.
  **b.** When Jeff spoke to Nathan, he said his computer battery was dead.
  **c.** Jeff told Nathan about his dead computer battery.
  **d.** Jeff told Nathan that the battery in Nathan's computer was dead.

For questions 17–19, choose the option that correctly completes the sentence.

**17.** The cat _____ in a patch of sun in front of the store.
  **a.** is laying
  **b.** is lying
  **c.** lays
  **d.** laid

**18.** At the start of the training session, Max _____ walked to the whiteboard and _____ wrote his name and email address.
a. calmly, carefully
b. calmly, careful
c. calm, careful
d. calm, carefully

**19.** _____ refunds will be made, unless the unworn product has visible defects, such as tears or _____.
a. know, wholes
b. know, holes
c. no, holes
d. no, wholes

**20.** Which of the following sentences contains a redundancy? (It repeats words that express the same idea.)
a. Please prepare the report carefully to avoid grammatical errors.
b. Twenty minutes had passed before the email arrived.
c. Yesterday, the senator made the same speech at three different locations.
d. For a wide variety of different reasons, more people are using laptop computers.

**21.** Which version has a parallel structure?

    **a.** He is a man of many talents. He balances the office budget, he is a skilled graphic designer, and you should see his grant proposals.

    **b.** He is a man of many talents. There's a talent for balancing the office budget, he is a skilled graphic designer, and then there are the grant proposals.

    **c.** He is a man of many talents. He balances the office budget, he is a skilled graphic designer, and he writes grant proposals.

    **d.** He is a man of many talents: balancing the office budget, doing graphic design, and he writes grant proposals.

**22.** Which of the following sentences contains a cliché?

    **a.** Looking for the old contract was like searching for a needle in a haystack.

    **b.** I can't meet at noon because I have a dentist appointment.

    **c.** The crooked fence looked like a row of teeth in need of braces.

    **d.** As costs go up, so do prices.

**23.** Which version is punctuated correctly?

    **a.** The defendant, breached her duty of care, to the plaintiff, when she failed to mop the floor.

    **b.** The defendant, breached her duty of care to the plaintiff, when she failed to mop the floor.

    **c.** The defendant breached her duty of care, to the plaintiff when she failed to mop the floor.

    **d.** The defendant breached her duty of care to the plaintiff when she failed to mop the floor.

**24.** Which version is correctly capitalized?
   **a.** Many Meteorologists are predicting that the West will have the wettest winter on record.
   **b.** Many meteorologists are predicting that the west will have the wettest winter on record.
   **c.** Many Meteorologists are predicting that the West will have the wettest Winter on record.
   **d.** Many meteorologists are predicting that the West will have the wettest winter on record.

**25.** Three of the following sentences are either run-ons or comma splices. Which one is NOT?
   **a.** I'm confused about why the account fell through let's arrange a time to discuss this.
   **b.** The candidate was scheduled for an interview at noon, he never showed up.
   **c.** Let's meet and go over the proposal, I have a few ideas.
   **d.** Karen arrived to work late, but she stayed an extra hour to make up for it.

**26.** Which version is punctuated correctly?
   **a.** There are many reasons—aside from the obvious ones— why she is not the right person for this job.
   **b.** There are many reasons: aside from the obvious ones— why she is not the right person for this job.
   **c.** There are many reasons—aside from the obvious ones, why she is not the right person for this job.
   **d.** There are many reasons aside from the obvious ones— why she is not the right person for this job.

**27.** Which is the correct punctuation for the underlined portion?

The explosion broke several windows in the <u>factory how-ever</u> no one was injured.

**a.** factory, however
**b.** factory however;
**c.** factory; however,
**d.** factory, however;

**28.** Which version uses hyphens correctly?
   **a.** The soft-spoken Vice-President did not raise his voice when he saw that his car had been damaged in the parking-lot.
   **b.** The soft spoken Vice-President did not raise his voice when he saw that his car had been damaged in the parking-lot.
   **c.** The soft-spoken Vice-President did not raise his voice when he saw that his car had been damaged in the parking lot.
   **d.** The soft-spoken vice president did not raise his voice when he saw that his car had been damaged in the parking lot.

**29.** Which version is punctuated correctly?
   **a.** Ms. Jeffers who is my assistant, previously worked in the IT Department.
   **b.** Ms. Jeffers, who is my assistant, previously worked in the IT Department.
   **c.** Ms. Jeffers who is my assistant, previously worked in the IT Department.
   **d.** Ms. Jeffers who, is my assistant, previously worked in the IT Department.

For questions 30–34, choose the option that correctly completes the sentence.

**30.** Several manuals, each with detailed instructions, _____ with your new computer.
    **a.** were sent
    **b.** was sent
    **c.** has been sent
    **d.** sent

**31.** Jessica and _____ are looking for the perfect image for the cover of the report; _____ will be hard to find.
    **a.** me, it
    **b.** me, they
    **c.** I, they
    **d.** I, it

**32.** Yesterday, I _____ my manuscript on this table, but now _____ gone.
    **a.** set, it's
    **b.** set, its
    **c.** sat, its
    **d.** sat, it's

**33.** I didn't want Lisa's _____ because I knew she would tell me not to _____ the proposal.
    **a.** advice, except
    **b.** advice, accept
    **c.** advise, accept
    **d.** advise, except

**34.** Carlos _____ the campaign because he had
_____ many other responsibilities.
- **a.** quite, too
- **b.** quite, to
- **c.** quit, to
- **d.** quit, too

**35.** Which version is punctuated correctly?
- **a.** The recreation center will show the following movies: *Charlotte's Web*, *The Jungle Book*, and *Annie*, the cost will be $2.50 per ticket.
- **b.** The recreation center will show the following movies; *Charlotte's Web*, *The Jungle Book*, and *Annie*; the cost will be $2.50 per ticket.
- **c.** The recreation center will show the following movies: *Charlotte's Web*, *The Jungle Book*, and *Annie*. The cost will be $2.50 per ticket.
- **d.** The recreation center will show the following movies— *Charlotte's Web*, *The Jungle Book*, and *Annie*. The cost will be $2.50 per ticket.

**36.** Which version is punctuated correctly?
- **a.** Excited about her meeting with the prospective client Eva spent hours preparing a detailed proposal.
- **b.** Excited about her meeting with the prospective client, Eva, spent hours preparing a detailed proposal.
- **c.** Excited about her meeting with the prospective client, Eva spent hours preparing a detailed proposal.
- **d.** Excited about her meeting with the prospective client Eva spent, hours preparing a detailed proposal.

**37.** Which version is punctuated correctly?
    **a.** The company first opened its doors on July 4, 1922, in Washington, D.C.
    **b.** The company, first opened its doors, on July 4, 1922, in Washington, D.C.
    **c.** The company first opened, its doors, on July 4, 1922 in Washington, D.C.
    **d.** The company first opened it's doors on July 4, 1922 in Washington D.C.

For question 38, choose the correct verb tense.

**38.** By next fall, I _____ all of our storage facilities.
    **a.** would have visited
    **b.** should have visited
    **c.** will have visited
    **d.** had visited

**39.** Three of the following sentences are punctuated correctly. Which one is punctuated incorrectly?
    **a.** The fundraiser was postponed; it was raining too hard.
    **b.** Because it was raining too hard; the fundraiser was postponed.
    **c.** The fundraiser was postponed because it was raining too hard.
    **d.** It was raining too hard, and the fundraiser was postponed.

**40.** Which of the following should NOT be hyphenated?
    **a.** one-fifteen in the afternoon
    **b.** the sixteenth-president of the United States
    **c.** a thirty-second commercial
    **d.** a thousand-dollar profit

**41.** In which of the following sentences is the underlined verb NOT in agreement with the subject of the sentence?

    **a.** There <u>is</u> only one manager at the store today.

    **b.** Why <u>are</u> the shipments arriving late?

    **c.** Here <u>are</u> the contracts I wanted to show you.

    **d.** What <u>is</u> the causes of the customer's complaints?

**42.** In which of the following sentences is the underlined pronoun incorrect?

    **a.** The team member who won the award was <u>her</u>.

    **b.** <u>He and I</u> plan to meet with you tomorrow.

    **c.** When can <u>she</u> come in for an interview?

    **d.** Both Michael and Steven will finish <u>their</u> reports by the end of the day.

**43.** Which version is punctuated correctly?

    **a.** Dianes' completed forms aren't in our files.

    **b.** Diane's completed forms are'nt in our files.

    **c.** Diane's completed forms' aren't in our files.

    **d.** Diane's completed forms aren't in our files.

**44.** Which version is written correctly?

    **a.** Mad Men was a popular television show about an advertising agency in the 1960s and 1970s.

    **b.** *Mad Men* was a popular television show about an advertising agency in the 1960s and 1970s.

    **c.** "Mad Men" was a popular television show about an advertising agency in the 1960s and 1970s.

    **d.** MAD MEN was a popular television show about an advertising agency in the 1960s and 1970s.

**45.** Which of the following sentences is in the passive voice?
   **a.** Every morning this week, Zeke brought bagels to work.
   **b.** Each day, he selected several different kinds.
   **c.** Generally, more than half of the bagels were eaten before 9:00.
   **d.** We've asked him to stop because we've all gained a few pounds.

**46.** We noticed the _____ of his cologne when he _____ our desks.
   **a.** scent, past
   **b.** scent, passed
   **c.** sent, passed
   **d.** sent, past

**47.** The Bridge Street location _____ of our express branches, but _____ all of our stores, it gets the highest ratings for customer service.
   **a.** smallest, among
   **b.** smallest, between
   **c.** smaller, between
   **d.** smaller, among

**48.** _____ the person _____ had the highest sales this month.
   **a.** Your, who
   **b.** Your, which
   **c.** You're, that
   **d.** You're, who

**49.** I _____ you would like the completed report sooner
rather _____ later.
   **a.** supposed, then
   **b.** suppose, then
   **c.** suppose, than
   **d.** supposed, than

**50.** Have you read _____ the proposal _____ ?
   **a.** through, all ready
   **b.** through, already
   **c.** threw, all ready
   **d.** threw, already

# Answers

**1.** Choice **b** is correct. This sentence does have a subject (*the managers and the support staff*) and a verb phrase (*had been called*). However, one word changes everything: *Although* is a conjunction, which tells you that this is a dependent clause. This dependent clause cannot stand alone as a sentence, so it is a sentence fragment.

Choice **a** is incorrect. This sentence has a subject (*The memo*) and a verb phrase (*was distributed*), so it is complete.

Choice **c** is incorrect. The sentence has a subject (*the company*) and a verb phrase (*was being acquired*), with no elements left hanging. This is a complete sentence.

Choice **d** is incorrect. This one is a bit trickier, as there seems to be a missing subject. However, in a case like this where the speaker is clearly addressing someone, *you* (or the listener) are the unspoken subject of the sentence. So if you look at the sentence as *You, be sure to attend the meeting*, it is complete.

**2.** Choice **b** is correct. *West* should be lowercase because it refers to a compass direction, not a particular region. *Ford Taurus* is a brand name, which is always capitalized.

Choice **a** is incorrect. *Interstate* should be capitalized, as it's the name of the highway.

Choice **c** is incorrect. *West* should not be capitalized because it refers to a compass direction here, not a specific place or geographic region.

Choice **d** is incorrect. *West* should not be capitalized because it refers to a compass direction here, not a specific place or geographic region. *Taurus* is part of a brand name (it's the name of the car), so it should be capitalized.

**3.** Choice **d** is correct. Restrictive clauses (which contain information essential to the sentence) do not require commas.
Choice **a** is incorrect. The comma is placed in a spot that creates two phrases that cannot stand on their own: *That building* and *with the copper dome is the state capitol.*
Choice **b** is incorrect. The comma is placed in a spot that creates two phrases that cannot stand on their own: *That building with the copper dome* and *is the state capitol.*
Choice **c** is incorrect. The comma placement suggests that the phrase *with the copper dome* is a nonrestrictive clause and could be removed from the sentence without changing its meaning. But without that phrase, how do you know which building *that* is?

**4.** Choice **a** is correct. Both *The temperature was 80 degrees at noon* and *by 6:00 P.M. it had dropped to below 40* are independent clauses. If there is no coordinating conjunction, a semicolon is needed to separate the two clauses.
Choice **b** is incorrect. Using a comma instead of a semicolon to separate two independent clauses creates a comma splice.
Choice **c** is incorrect. This choice is a run-on sentence because two independent clauses are run together. In addition, the comma after *6 P.M.* is unnecessary and confusing.
Choice **d** is incorrect. This is a run-on sentence.

**5.** Choice **c** is correct. Both *manager* and *month* are correctly treated as singular possessives (with the apostrophe before the *s*).
Choice **a** is incorrect. The sentence tells you that it was one person's idea, but *managers'* (with the apostrophe following the *s*) is plural.
Choice **b** is incorrect. *Manager's* is correct, but *months* is plural when it should be possessive. (The sentence says that the time period in question is *a* month.)
Choice **d** is incorrect. *Managers* is a plural noun, but the adjective *one* indicates that it should be singular.

**6.** Choice **b** is correct. The tag is separated from the quotation, and the punctuation marks are correctly placed within the quotation marks.

Choice **a** is incorrect. This choice is missing quotation marks within the sentence to let the reader know where the police officer's direct quote begins and ends. *Yelled the police officer* is a tag, or a speaker identifier, which is separate from the actual quotation.

Choice **c** is incorrect. End marks like exclamation points should always be placed within a quotation mark if they are part of the statement.

Choice **d** is incorrect. The second quotation mark is placed incorrectly after *officer*. When you read the sentence, think about what makes sense for the quotation: Is it likely that the speaker actually said, "yelled the police officer"? That can help you figure out where the quotation marks should be.

**7.** Choice **a** is correct. In this case, the parentheses surround a side comment that can be removed from the sentence without affecting its meaning. It offers extra information that isn't directly related to the instructions.

Choice **b** is incorrect. Parentheses are used to surround a side comment that is nonessential to the sentence's meaning. If you remove the parenthetical information in this sentence, you're left with an incomplete thought.

Choice **c** is incorrect. Parentheses are used to surround a side comment that is nonessential to the sentence's meaning. If you remove the parenthetical information in this sentence, you're left with an incomplete thought.

Choice **d** is incorrect. Parentheses are used to surround a side comment that is nonessential to the sentence's meaning. If you remove the parenthetical information in this sentence, you're left with an incomplete thought.

**8.** Choice **d** is correct. *Two* is a plural subject, so it agrees with the plural verb *have arrived.*

Choice **a** is incorrect. *Each* is a singular pronoun, but the verb *have arrived* is plural.

Choice **b** is incorrect. *Neither* is a singular pronoun, so it requires a singular verb. However, the verb *have arrived* is plural.

Choice **c** is incorrect. *One* is a singular pronoun, and the verb *have arrived* is plural, so the subject should be plural.

**9.** Choice **c** is correct. This sentence is divided into two proper clauses: a dependent clause setting the scene (*As we waited for the conference call to begin*), and an independent clause describing the action (*Bart told us about the proposal he pitched*). It clearly expresses the actual meaning of the sentence.

Choice **a** is incorrect. In this sentence, it's unclear whether Bart pitched the proposal while he was waiting for the conference call to begin, or if he was telling the story while waiting for the conference call to begin.

Choice **b** is incorrect. In this sentence, it's unclear whether Bart pitched the proposal while he was waiting for the call, or if he was telling the story while waiting for the call.

Choice **d** is incorrect. This sentence makes it sound like Bart pitched the proposal while waiting for the conference call to begin, which is not the correct meaning.

**10.** Choice **a** is correct. The action verb *requested* makes it clear that this sentence is in active voice.

Choice **b** is incorrect. *Donations had been requested* contains a passive verb phrase. Note the additional verbs that separating the subject (*Donations*) and the active verb (*requested*).

Choice **c** is incorrect. *Donations . . . were requested* contains a passive verb phrase. Note the additional verb separating the subject (*Donations*) and the active verb (*requested*).

Choice **d** is incorrect. *Donations were requested* contains a passive verb phrase. Note the additional verb separating the subject (*Donations*) and the active verb (*requested*).

**11.** Choice **c** is correct. The perspective stays in the first person throughout the entire sentence (*we*/*us*/*we*).

Choice **a** is incorrect. This choice starts with the first person (*We went canoeing . . .*) but then switches over to the second person (*You could see . . .*).

Choice **b** is incorrect. This choice starts with the first person (*While we were canoeing . . .*) but then switches over to the second person (*you could see . . .*).

Choice **d** is incorrect. This choice starts with the second person (*down at you . . .*) but then switches over to the first person (*we canoed . . .*).

**12.** Choice **b** is correct. Both the exclamation and the question have the appropriate punctuation.

Choice **a** is incorrect. The sentence, *Do you know where I can find a website developer on short notice* is a question and should end with a question mark.

Choice **c** is incorrect. *Help* is an interjection, not a question, and should end with an exclamation point. *Do you know where I can find a website developer on short notice* is a question for the reader, not an exclamatory statement.

Choice **d** is incorrect. The question is punctuated correctly, but the interjection *Help* should end with an exclamation point.

**13.** Choice **c** is correct. If the sentence talked about *a* university or *the* university, the word would not be capitalized. But the sentence mentions a specific university. *University* is part of the full name and should be capitalized.

Choice **a** is incorrect. *Professor* is not used as a name here, so it should not be capitalized.

Choice **b** is incorrect. *History* is a general subject in this case, not a specific class, so it should not be capitalized.

Choice **d** is incorrect. *Fall* is used generically here to describe the season, so it should not be capitalized.

**14.** Choice **d** is correct. *Chose* is the correct past tense of the verb *choose* and agrees with the rest of the sentence.

Choice **a** is incorrect. *Has chosen* is the present perfect tense, which expresses a past event in the present. However, the rest of the sentence is in the past tense, so the verb should be past tense.

Choice **b** is incorrect. *Choosed* is not a word.

Choice **c** is incorrect. *Choose* is a present-tense verb, but the verb *was asked* is past tense. The two verbs must agree and both be in the past tense.

**15.** Choice **a** is correct. *Yesterday afternoon* tells you that the action takes place in the past, so a past-tense verb is needed. *Began* is the past tense of the verb *begin*.

Choice **b** is incorrect. *Begun* is the past participle of *begin*, not the past tense. The past participle is generally preceded by *has/have/had*, which is not part of this sentence.

Choice **c** is incorrect. This is a past participial phrase, but it has the wrong past participle.

Choice **d** is incorrect. *Yesterday afternoon* tells you that the action takes place in the past, so a past-tense verb is needed. *Begins* is a present-tense verb.

**16.** Choice **d** is correct. It may seem like overkill to use Nathan's name twice in one sentence, but when both Nathan and Jeff could be the antecedent of the pronoun *he*, you need to be as specific as possible about who is doing what.

Choice **a** is incorrect. The antecedent of the pronoun *his* is unclear in this sentence: Does *his* refer to the subject (*Jeff*) or the object (*Nathan*)? It's unclear whose battery is dead.

Choice **b** is incorrect. The antecedents of the pronouns *he* and *his* are unclear, so you don't know which person corresponds to what pronoun.

Choice **c** is incorrect. The antecedent of the pronoun *his* is unclear: did Jeff tell Nathan about Jeff's dead battery or Nathan's dead battery?

**17.** Choice **b** is correct. *Lying* is the correct present participle of *lie.*

Choice **a** is incorrect. While similar, *lay* actually means *to put* or *to set*, while *lie* means *to recline*. It's much more likely that the cat is *reclining* in front of the store rather than being *set* there, so *laying* is incorrect.

Choice **c** is incorrect. The present tense verb *lays* does not have the correct meaning in the context of this sentence.

Choice **d** is incorrect. *Laid* is the past participle of *lay*, which does not have the correct meaning in the context of this sentence.

**18.** Choice **a** is correct. Both of the blanks must be filled with adverbs because they modify two verbs (*walked* and *wrote*). Both *calmly* and *carefully* are adverbs that correctly complete the sentence.

Choice **b** is incorrect. Both of the blanks must be filled with adverbs because they modify two verbs (*walked* and *wrote*). *Careful* is an adjective (it modifies a noun, not a verb).

Choice **c** is incorrect. Both of the blanks must be filled with adverbs because they modify two verbs (*walked* and *wrote*). *Calm* and *careful* are adjectives.

Choice **d** is incorrect. Both of the blanks must be filled with adverbs because they modify two verbs (*walked* and *wrote*). *Calm* is an adjective.

**19.** Choice **c** is correct. *No* is used as an adjective to modify *refunds*, and *holes* is the correct noun in the context of the sentence.

Choice **a** is incorrect. The first blank must be filled with an adjective that describes *refunds*. *Know* is a verb. Also, *wholes* is incorrect.

Choice **b** is incorrect. The first blank must be filled with an adjective that describes *refunds*. *Know* is a verb.

Choice **d** is incorrect. *Holes* describes a defect, not *wholes*.

**20.** Choice **d** is correct. The quickest indicator of redundancy is when synonyms appear multiple times in a sentence, as with *variety* and *different* in this sentence. Both words are expressing the same thing. A less redundant sentence would read, *For a wide variety of reasons . . .* or *For different reasons. . . .*

Choice **a** is incorrect. This sentence has no conflict or redundancy among its elements.

Choice **b** is incorrect. This sentence has no conflict or redundancy among its elements.

Choice **c** is incorrect. This sentence has no conflict or redundancy among its elements.

**21.** Choice **c** is correct. The pronoun *he* is applied to each part of the sentence; also, the tenses are used consistently (*he balances . . . he is . . . he writes*).

Choice **a** is incorrect. This sentence uses the pronoun *he* to list his accomplishments, then switches to *you*, which changes the point of view from third person to second person.

Choice **b** is incorrect. This sentence switches from the direct pronoun *he* to a passive voice that removes him from the action.

Choice **d** is incorrect. The tense shifts from the present perfect (*balancing, doing*) to the simple present (*writes*).

**22.** Choice **a** is correct. The *needle in a haystack* is a phrase we've all heard countless times to describe a task that is difficult.

Choice **b** is incorrect. A dentist's appointment may be an excuse, but it's not a common, overused expression.

Choice **c** is incorrect. The fence and crooked teeth are a simile, or a comparison based on the writer's observation.

Choice **d** is incorrect. This is a principle or a concept. It is not an example of a cliché.

**23.** Choice **d** is correct. This sentence does not contain any unnecessary commas.

Choice **a** is incorrect. *Breached her duty of care* and *to the plaintiff* are essential to the sentence and should not be set off by commas.

Choice **b** is incorrect. *Breached her care of duty to the plaintiff* is essential to the sentence and should not be set off by commas.

Choice **c** is incorrect. A comma should not appear after the word *care*.

**24.** Choice **d** is correct. The only proper noun in the sentence is *West*, as it refers to a specific region and not just a compass direction.

Choice **a** is incorrect. In this sentence, *meteorologists* refers to a generic group of meteorologists, not a specific title. It is not a proper noun and should not be capitalized.

Choice **b** is incorrect. Because *west* refers to a specific region in this sentence (suggested by the use of *the*), it should be capitalized.

Choice **c** is incorrect. *Meteorologists* is not a proper noun, so it should not be capitalized. In addition, *winter* should not be capitalized when it describes the season in general.

**25.** Choice **d** is correct. In this sentence, two independent clauses are joined by a comma and a conjunction (*but*).

Choice **a** is incorrect. This sentence is a run-on because it contains two independent clauses that are not separated with punctuation.

Choice **b** is incorrect. This sentence is a comma splice because it separates the two independent clauses with a comma but no conjunction.

Choice **c** is incorrect. This sentence is a comma splice because it separates the two independent clauses with a comma but no conjunction.

**26.** Choice **a** is correct. The em-dashes are used to separate the side comment from the rest of the sentence.

Choice **b** is incorrect. Rather than a colon, a second em-dash is needed to set off the comment within the sentence.

Choice **c** is incorrect. Rather than a comma, the second em-dash when setting off a comment within the sentence.

Choice **d** is incorrect. While an em-dash can be used to create a dramatic pause in a sentence, there's no reason to pause in this spot. It separates the same idea into two unnecessarily different parts.

**27.** Choice **c** is correct. *However* is a conjunctive adverb, which should be accompanied by a semicolon. In this case, *however* is also an introductory clause, so it is followed by a comma. Choice **a** is incorrect. Using a comma here creates a comma splice.

Choice **b** is incorrect. The adverb *however* should come after the semicolon because it belongs to the second independent clause.

Choice **d** is incorrect. Because *however* is a conjunctive adverb, it should be preceded by a semicolon, not a comma. Also, it is an introductory clause and should be followed by a comma.

**28.** Choice **c** is correct. *Soft-spoken* and *vice-president* should both be hyphenated because they form a single adjective and a single noun, respectively.

Choice **a** is incorrect. *Soft-spoken* (a compound adjective) and *vice-president* (a compound noun) are hyphenated correctly, but *parking lot* should not be hyphenated.

Choice **b** is incorrect. Because *soft-spoken* is used as a single compound word to modify *vice-president*, it should be hyphenated.

Choice **d** is incorrect. *Vice-president* is a compound noun, and must be hyphenated.

**29.** Choice **b** is correct. The dependent phrase *who is my assistant* is correctly set off by commas.

Choice **a** is incorrect. The phrase *who is my assistant* is a nonrestrictive clause (it offers additional information but is not crucial to the meaning of the sentence), so it should be preceded and followed by commas.

Choice **c** is incorrect. The phrase *who is my assistant* is not crucial to the meaning of the sentence, so it should be preceded and followed by commas.

Choice **d** is incorrect. This choice puts commas around the wrong clause. If you take out the words between the commas, you're left with *Ms. Jeffers who previously worked in the IT Department*. This is a sentence fragment

**30.** Choice **a** is correct. *Were sent* is the correct past-tense verb phrase to modify the plural subject *several manuals*.

Choice **b** is incorrect. *Was sent* is a singular verb phrase, which does not agree with the plural subject *several manuals*.

Choice **c** is incorrect. *Has been sent* is a singular verb phrase, which does not agree with the plural subject *several manuals*.

Choice **d** is incorrect. *Sent* is the past participle of *send*, and it agrees with the tense of the sentence. However, *sent* is not the correct verb because it is missing the past form of *to be* (*were*).

**31.** Choice **d** is correct. It uses the nominative case pronoun *I* correctly, and *it* is the pronoun consistent with the phrase it's modifying (*the perfect image*).

Choice **a** is incorrect. *Me* is an objective-case pronoun, but in this sentence it is acting as the subject, which requires the nominative case pronoun *I*.

Choice **b** is incorrect. *Me* is an objective-case pronoun, but in this sentence it is acting as the subject, which requires a nominative case pronoun. Also, *they* is incorrect because the clause modifies *the perfect image*.

Choice **c** is incorrect. *I* is the correct pronoun when referring to oneself as a subject; however, *they* should be singular to match *the perfect image*.

**32.** Choice **a** is correct. *Set*, meaning *to put* or *to place*, is the correct verb in the context of the sentence. *It's*, a contraction meaning *it is*, is also correct.

Choice **b** is incorrect. *Its* is a possessive pronoun that is being used incorrectly. The contraction *it's* (to replace *it is*) should be used.

Choice **c** is incorrect. *Sat* is the past participle of *sit*, which means *to rest*; you want a verb that means *to put*. Additionally, *its* is a possessive pronoun.

Choice **d** is incorrect. *Sat* is the past participle of *sit*, which means *to rest*; you want a verb that means *to put*.

**33.** Choice **b** is correct. *Advice* is a noun, which fits the structure and meaning of the sentence. *Accept* is the correct verb.

Choice **a** is incorrect. The two blanks must be filled with a noun and a verb, respectively. *Except* is a preposition meaning *excluding*.

Choice **c** is incorrect. *Advise* is a verb that means *to give advice*; the first blank requires a noun.

Choice **d** is incorrect. *Advise* is a verb that means *to give advice*; the first blank requires a noun. *Except* is a preposition, not the verb needed to fill in the second blank.

**34.** Choice **d** is correct. The verb *quit* works in the context of the sentence, and the adverb *too* (meaning *excessive*) successfully modifies *many*.

Choice **a** is incorrect. Based on the context of the sentence, the first blank requires a verb (what did Carlos do?). *Quite* is an adverb.

Choice **b** is incorrect. Based on the context of the sentence, the first blank requires a verb (what did Carlos do?). *Quite* is an adverb. *To* is also incorrect, as it is a preposition and the second blank requires an adverb.

Choice **c** is incorrect. The preposition *to* is not an adverb to modify the phrase *many other responsibilities.*

**35.** Choice **c** is correct. The list of movies is punctuated correctly (beginning with a colon and separating list items with commas). This choice also splits the two independent clauses into separate sentences with a period.

Choice **a** is incorrect. The comma after *Annie* (with no coordinating conjunction) turns the sentence into a comma splice.

Choice **b** is incorrect. A list should be preceded by a colon, not a semicolon.

Choice **d** is incorrect. The list should be preceded by a colon, not an em-dash, because it is an essential component of the sentence.

**36.** Choice **c** is correct. The comma separates the introductory phrase from the independent clause that follows it.

Choice **a** is incorrect. *Excited about her meeting with the prospective client* is an introductory phrase and should be followed by a comma.

Choice **b** is incorrect. The comma before *Eva* is correct, but the following comma is incorrect because *Eva* is the subject of the sentence.

Choice **d** is incorrect. This comma breaks the sentence into two pieces that make little sense: *Excited about her meeting with one prospective client Eva spent* and *hours preparing a detailed proposal.*

**37.** Choice **a** is correct. When dates come in the middle of a sentence, they should be followed by commas (as *July 4* and *1922* are here). There should also be a comma between a city name and a state (or U.S. district) abbreviation.
Choice **b** is incorrect. This sentence sets off *first opened its doors* as a nonrestrictive phrase, when it's essential to the sentence.
Choice **c** is incorrect. The comma after *opened* creates a false pause in the sentence and separates it into two separate phrases.
Choice **d** is incorrect. This sentence uses the contraction *it's* instead of the possessive *its*.

**38.** Choice **c** is correct. When speculating about future events, you should use the future perfect tense. *Will have been* is the future perfect form of the verb *to be*.
Choice **a** is incorrect. While the sentence does indicate the future (*By next fall*), the tense you're looking for is the future perfect, which describes an expected event that hasn't yet taken place. *Would be* is the future tense, but it is not the future perfect tense.
Choice **b** is incorrect. The sentence indicates the future (*By next fall*). However, *should have* is a verb phrase that refers to past events that may have happened, or events that did not happen.
Choice **d** is incorrect. The sentence indicates the future (*By next fall*). However, *had been* is the past perfect tense, which is used to describe events that have already happened.

**39.** Choice **b** is correct. An introductory clause like *Because it was raining too hard* should be followed by a comma, not a semicolon.

Choice **a** is incorrect. This sentence is correctly punctuated because the semicolon separates two distinct (but related) ideas: that the fundraiser was postponed and that it was raining.

Choice **c** is incorrect. This sentence is correctly punctuated because the word *because* links the independent and dependent clauses with no additional punctuation necessary.

Choice **d** is incorrect. This sentence is correctly punctuated because the two independent clauses are joined by a comma and the conjunction *and*.

**40.** Choice **b** is correct. *Sixteenth* is not part of a compound adjective; it is the only word modifying the noun *president*. There does not need to be a hyphen between a noun and its modifier.

Choice **a** is incorrect. When time is written out in words, the hour and the minute should be hyphenated.

Choice **c** is incorrect. A compound adjective containing a number (*thirty*) and a word (*second*) should be hyphenated.

Choice **d** is incorrect. A compound adjective containing a number (*thousand*) and a word (*dollar*) should be hyphenated.

**41.** Choice **d** is correct. The verb (*is*) is singular, while the subject (*causes*) is plural. The subject and verb are not in agreement.

Choice **a** is incorrect. *One* is a singular pronoun, so the singular verb *is* is correct.

Choice **b** is incorrect. *Shipments* is a plural noun, so the plural verb *are* is correct.

Choice **c** is incorrect. *Contracts* is a plural noun, so the plural verb *are* is correct.

**42.** Choice **a** is correct. The pronoun here is deceptive. It might appear to be an object of *team member*, but it is actually a predicate noun renaming the subject of the sentence. The correct nominative pronoun is *she*.

Choice **b** is incorrect. The pronouns here are used as the subjects of the sentence (who plans to meet with you tomorrow?), and *he* and *I* are both nominative-case pronouns.

Choice **c** is incorrect. Although it comes in the middle of the sentence, *she* is the subject of the sentence (*she* is the one performing the action of coming in). *She* is the correct nominative-case pronoun.

Choice **d** is incorrect. *Michael and Steven* make up the compound subject, and the coordinating word *and* tells you that the subject is plural. *Their* is the correct objective-case pronoun to match the plural subject.

**43.** Choice **d** is correct. *Diane* is correctly punctuated, there are no extraneous apostrophes in the sentence, and *aren't* is contracted properly.

Choice **a** is incorrect. *Diane* is one person, so the possessive form is created by adding *'s*.

Choice **b** is incorrect. *Diane's* is punctuated correctly, but the contraction *aren't* requires an apostrophe. Contractions with *not* always have the apostrophe between the *n* and the *t*.

Choice **c** is incorrect. *Forms* is a plural noun and is not possessive, so it should not contain an apostrophe.

**44.** Choice **b** is correct. The television show title is appropriately italicized.

Choice **a** is incorrect. Television show titles should be italicized, not underlined.

Choice **c** is incorrect. Television show titles should be italicized, not punctuated with quotation marks.

Choice **d** is incorrect. There is no reason to put television show titles in all-capital letters.

**45.** Choice **d** is correct. *Half of the bagels were eaten* contains a passive verb phrase. Note the additional verb separating the subject (*half*) and the active verb (*eaten*). The active sentence would be, *We ate more than half of the bagels before 9:00.*

Choice **a** is incorrect. The subject (*Zeke*) directly performs the action (*brought*), so this is an active sentence.

Choice **b** is incorrect. The subject (*Zeke*) directly performs the action (*selected*), so this is an active sentence.

Choice **d** is incorrect. The subject (*we*) is directly performing the action (*asked*), so this is an active sentence.

**46.** Choice **b** is correct. *Scent* is the correct noun for this sentence, and *passed* is the correct past-tense verb.

Choice **a** is incorrect. Based on the context of the sentence, the two blanks must be filled with a noun and a verb, respectively. *Scent* is the correct noun, but *past* can be either a noun or an adjective—not a verb.

Choice **c** is incorrect. *Sent* is a verb, but a noun is needed to serve as the direct object.

Choice **d** is incorrect. Based on the context of the sentence, the two blanks must be filled with a noun and a verb, respectively. However, *sent* is a verb, and *past* can be either an adjective or a noun.

**47.** Choice **a** is correct. The adjective *smallest* indicates that the Bridge Street store is small compared to the two other express branches. *Among* indicates that its customer service ratings are those for multiple stores.

Choice **b** is incorrect. *Between* compares two items. Since there are at least three branches, more than two things are being compared, so the comparative adverb is incorrect.

Choice **c** is incorrect. *Smaller* and *between* compare two items. Since there are at least three branches, these comparative adverbs are incorrect.

Choice **d** is incorrect. *Smaller* compares two items. Since there are at least three branches, the comparative adverb is incorrect.

**48.** Choice **d** is correct. The contraction *you're* is appropriate for the first blank, and *who* correctly modifies *the person*.

Choice **a** is incorrect. The first blank of the sentence is missing the subject and the verb. *You're* (contraction of *you* are) fits that space; the possessive pronoun *your* does not.

Choice **b** is incorrect. The first blank of the sentence is missing the subject and the verb. *You're* (contraction of *you* are) fits that space; the possessive pronoun *your* does not. Also, the second blank of the subject is asking for a pronoun to complete the object. *Which* is a pronoun, but it describes an object or idea, never a person.

Choice **c** is incorrect. *That* is incorrect because it is an object pronoun for inanimate things; it never modifies a person.

**49.** Choice **c** is correct. *Suppose* is the correct verb tense, and the meaning of *than* (showing that sooner is better compared to later) fits the sentence as well.

Choice **a** is incorrect. *Would like* indicates present tense; therefore, the past-tense verb *supposed* is not correct. *Then* is also not correct because it is an adverb that modifies time. The second blank requires a conjunction that shows a comparison of one thing to another.

Choice **b** is incorrect. The second blank requires a conjunction that shows a comparison of one thing to another. *Then* is an adverb that modifies time.

Choice **d** is incorrect. *Would like* indicates present tense; therefore, the past-tense verb *supposed* is not correct.

**50.** Choice **b** is correct. *Through* correctly introduces a prepositional phrase. The adverb *already* means *by this time*.

Choice **a** is incorrect. *All ready*, which means completely ready, doesn't make sense in the context of the sentence.

Choice **c** is incorrect. The verb *threw* doesn't make sense in the context of the sentence. In addition, *all ready*, which means completely ready, is incorrect.

Choice **d** is incorrect. The verb *threw* doesn't make sense in the context of the sentence.

# GLOSSARY

**action verb**  a verb that expresses thought or activity

**adjective**  a word that modifies a noun or a pronoun; adjectives answer *what kind? which one? how much? how many?* about a noun

**adverb**  a word that modifies a verb, an adjective, or another adverb; adverbs answer *where? when? how much? how many?* about the verb, adjective, or other adverb

**chronological order**  an organizational structure that presents events in sequence, or in the time order in which they happened

**colloquialism**  an informal word or phrase

**colon (:)**  the punctuation mark that comes before a series, a lengthy quotation, or an example or after the salutation in a business letter

**comma (,)**  the punctuation mark that separates words, phrases, and items in a series; commas are also used in compound and complex sentences to separate clauses

**compare**  to look for ways in which things are alike

**complex sentence**   a sentence that is made up of an independent clause and a dependent (subordinate) clause

**compound-complex sentence**   a sentence that is made up of more than one independent clause and at least one dependent clause

**compound sentence**   a sentence that contains at least two independent clauses with no dependent clauses

**compound subject**   two or more nouns that share the same verb in a sentence

**compound word**   two or more separate words put together to create a new word; compound words may be joined, separate, or hyphenated

**conclusion**   the final paragraph (or paragraphs) in an essay, which restates the main idea, summarizes the main points, and closes, sometimes with a call to action or an appeal to the reader's emotions

**conjunction**   a word or phrase (such as *and, or, but*) that connects words or groups of words

**contrast**   to show how things or ideas are different

**dangling modifier**   a word or phrase that is meant to modify a specific part of the sentence but has been misplaced, often resulting in confusion

**demonstrative pronoun**   a word (such as *this, that, these,* and *those*) used to replace a noun in a sentence

**dependent clause**   a group of words that cannot stand alone as a complete thought; also known as a *subordinate clause*

**direct object**   the noun or pronoun that receives the action of the verb

**direct quotation**   a person's exact spoken or written words, which must be enclosed in quotation marks (see also *indirect quotation*)

**effect**   what happens as a result of something else

**emoticon**   the typed representation of a facial expression; often used in emails

**emotional appeal**   an argument that appeals to the reader's emotions

**exclamation point (!)**   the punctuation mark that indicates strong emotion

**freewriting**   the practice of writing continuously without correcting spelling, grammar, or sentence structure to facilitate finding a topic or increase fluency; also called *prewriting*

**future tense**   a verb tense that indicates that something has not yet happened but will

**hyphen (-)**   punctuation mark that joins compound words

**indefinite pronoun**   a word such as *no one, anyone, anybody,* or *somebody* that refers to a nonspecific noun

**independent clause**   a group of words that contains a subject and a predicate (verb) and can stand by itself as a sentence

**indirect quotation**   what someone said, retold in your own words

**infinitive**   a verb written in the form of **to** plus **the verb** (for example, *to walk*) that acts as a noun, an adjective, or an adverb in a sentence

**interrogative pronouns**   a pronoun that asks *who, whom, whose,* and so on

**introduction**   a text's opening paragraph that hooks the reader and introduces the main idea

**irony**   saying the opposite of what you mean, usually for a humorous effect

**main idea**   what a selection is mostly about

**misplaced modifier**   a word or phrase that is placed too far from the noun or verb it is modifying, thus altering or confusing the meaning of the sentence

**modifier**   a word that describes or clarifies another word (see also *adjective* and *adverb*)

**noun**   a word that names a person, place, or thing (including ideas and feelings)

**object of a preposition**   the noun or pronoun that follows a prepositional phrase

**order of importance**   an organizational strategy that arranges ideas according to how important they are

**parentheses** [( )]   the punctuation marks that set off information that is not necessarily pertinent to the surrounding sentence or words

**participle**   a verb form that can be used as an adjective or a noun

**past tense**   a verb tense that indicates that something has already happened

**period** (.)   the punctuation mark found at the end of sentences and in abbreviations

**personal pronoun**   a word such as *I, you, me, he, him, she, her, it, they, them,* and *we* that refers to the speaker, the person, or the thing being spoken about

**phrase**   a group of words that does not have a subject and verb; phrases can act like various parts of speech (a noun, a verb, an adjective, an adverb, or a preposition)

**point of view**   the first-person, second-person, or third-person perspective from which something is written, or the opinion or position on a topic from which an author writes

**predicate**   the action that the subject performs in a sentence; a verb

**present tense**   a verb tense that indicates action happening in the present or an action that happens constantly

**prewriting**   the practice of writing continuously without correcting spelling, grammar, or sentence structure to facilitate generating ideas; also called *freewriting*

**pronoun**   a part of speech that takes the place of a noun in a sentence

**proper noun**   a specific noun that is capitalized

**punctuation**   a set of grammatical symbols used in written language to indicate the ends of clauses or sentences

**question mark** (?)   the punctuation mark that appears at the end of an interrogatory sentence (a question)

**quotation marks** (" ")   the punctuation marks that indicate the exact words of a speaker being quoted; sometimes quotation marks are used to convey a satiric or ironic intent in the author's words

**run-on sentence**  a sentence in which two or more complete sentences have been improperly joined together

**sarcasm**  bitter, derisive language

**semicolon (;)**  the punctuation mark that joins two independent clauses that share a similar idea and are not already joined by a conjunction

**sentence**  a group of words that has a subject and a predicate and expresses a complete thought

**sentence fragment**  an incomplete thought that has been punctuated as a complete sentence

**simple sentence**  an independent clause

**subject**  topic, or what the text is about; also, the grammatical term for the main noun in a sentence

**subject-verb agreement**  the rule that the subject and verb of a sentence must agree in number and in person

**subordinate clause**  a group of words that cannot stand alone as a complete thought; also known as a *dependent clause*

**thesis**  a statement in an essay that conveys the main idea

**tone**  the writer's style that reveals the attitudes and point of view of the author toward the topic

**topic**  the subject or main idea of an essay or a paragraph

**topic sentence**  a sentence that expresses the main idea of a paragraph

**verb**  a part of speech that expresses action or state of being. The tense of a verb indicates the time in which the verb takes place

# APPENDIX I: INTERVIEWING FOR SUCCESS ▶

The job search process can be a time-consuming one. After you have found the right job opportunities to apply for, and then submitted a well-written cover letter and a finely tuned resume to capture the potential employer's attention, then it is *your* responsibility to impress the person who invites you in for a job interview. Only after a successful interview might you receive a job offer.

This appendix introduces you to the different types of interviews used in the professional world and provides essential guidelines to follow as you prepare for great interviews.

Throughout each of your interviews, there will probably be a lot on your mind. What will be on the interviewer's mind, however, are these questions:

- Will this person be successful in the job if he or she is hired?
- Will this person be an asset to the company?

- Is this person worth the salary the company would be paying him or her?

Everything you do during an interview should help answer these questions in a positive way.

If you are nervous, don't worry. This appendix is designed to help you prepare for different job interview styles, conduct yourself professionally during any interview situation, and evaluate any job offer you receive.

## Creating a Great Impression

Being invited to participate in a job interview is a positive indication that your cover letter and resume have done their job. The experience and skills you displayed on paper have gotten a company interested in the possibility of hiring you. Now the employer wants to meet you in person, get to know you better, and learn more about your qualifications.

A job interview is your opportunity to sell yourself directly to a potential employer. From the moment you step into an employer's office, everything about you will be evaluated, including all of the following:

- appearance (personal grooming)
- attitude
- outfit
- body language
- personality
- communication skills
- level of preparation

The job interview is your big chance to impress the interviewer with everything you have to offer. It is your opportunity to set yourself apart from the other applicants, demonstrate that you are qualified to fill the available job opening, and show how excited you are about the prospect of working for that employer.

# Scheduling the Interview

Ideally, shortly after you send your resume and a cover letter to a potential employer, your telephone will ring (or a message will pop up in your inbox) and you will be invited in for an interview. When you are on the phone with a representative from the company, always act professionally and remember to obtain the information you need from the person with whom you are speaking. If your prospective employer reaches out over email, make sure you are just as professional and poised as you would be over the phone—see Chapter 6: Emails for more specific tips for formatting and tone.

There are four important rules for scheduling your interview:

1. **Be easy to schedule.** The interviewer, or his or her assistant, will likely start off the scheduling chat with a date. Try to be flexible. If she says "next Thursday at 3:00 P.M.," and that's when your weekly staff meeting takes place, reply with a better time for you, such as "next Thursday at lunchtime." However, watch how you say it. Don't be too specific, such as, "next Thursday at 12:15"—keep "lunchtime" open to his or her interpretation. Likewise, if before 9:00 A.M. is the best time for you, go ahead and say so, but if that time slot doesn't work for the interviewer, offer another one, such as during your lunch hour or after 5:00 P.M.

2. **Keep your scheduling details organized.** A person can be so excited, thrilled, or nervous about getting called for an interview that he or she can forget or misunderstand the details. First, pause and collect yourself. Then, thank the person on the other end of the phone line for calling, and ask for a moment to grab a pen and paper along with your planner.

3. **Remember your manners.** You never know who will have a say in the hiring decision, so why risk your future by using bad manners? Often, when a potential employer or human resources representative calls you to talk about setting up an interview, he or she is getting a sense of your personality over the phone.

4. **Schedule your interview with plenty of time to prepare.** Always avoid scheduling an interview for the same day that you are called to schedule an interview. Allow yourself at least one day, preferably two, to prepare and do your research.

## ⤷ TIPS

Here is a list of information you need to get during the initial interview scheduling call:

- the name of the person conducting the interview (along with his or her title)
- the exact position for which you are interviewing
- the location of the interview
- directions to the location (or make a note to yourself to Google directions ahead of time)
- the name of the person to ask for at the interview location, as well as that person's phone number and extension
- what additional materials, if any, to bring (such as a portfolio, samples, or reel)

At the end of the conversation, it is essential to do two things:

- confirm date, time, place, and materials to bring
- say "thank you"

## Dos and Don'ts

Here are some examples of the right and wrong way to schedule an interview with a potential employer.

### Scheduling the Right Way and Wrong Way: Example 1

**Wrong:** *Yeah, I can come in some time next week, I guess.*

**Wrong:** *Who? Oh, right. The marketing job. Uh, I'm not sure what my day looks like on Tuesday. Where's my iPhone? Let me call you back. . . .*

**Wrong:** *Wednesday? I'm supposed to go out of town tomorrow— can I get back to you in like a week or two?*

**Wrong:** *Smrrrring. Bhaah . . . . [inaudible or mumbled responses]*

**Right:** *Thank you for calling, Ms. Peterson. I am very interested in meeting with you to discuss the open position in the marketing department. I have several times available this week—are mornings or afternoons more convenient for you?*

### Scheduling the Right Way and Wrong Way: Example 2
**Wrong:** *Uh, okay, see you then. [Click.]*
**Wrong:** *Thanks. Bye.*
**Wrong:** *I hope to see you then. Ciao.*

**Right:** *Next Thursday, November 14th at 12:30 sounds perfect. I will see you at Milford Corporate Park in Human Resources reception, and I will bring my portfolio. Thanks again. Goodbye.*

### Scheduling the Right Way and Wrong Way: Example 3
**Wrong:** *Um, 3:00 P.M. is no good.*
**Wrong:** *I can't make it.*
**Wrong:** *Jeez, that's my kickboxing class time, and I always spend my lunch hour in that class on Mondays.*

**Right:** *Sorry, I have a staff meeting at that time. Does a bit earlier in the day work for you? I can come in around lunchtime.*

## CAUTION!

Keep in mind that the scheduling phone call or email is often a part of the screening process. If your attitude was rude, shy, or negative in any way, it was probably noted. An overly casual or blasé email will not get your interviewer excited about meeting with you, but on the other hand, your positive qualities will also be noted, so always be professional and respond in a timely manner.

# Pre-Interview Research

The first step when preparing for any interview is to do research. Always enter the interview knowing as much as possible about the employer and the related industry. Specifically, here are some of the details about which you want up-to-date and accurate information:

- **The job for which you are applying.** Know exactly what position you are hoping to fill, what the requirements are for that position, what skills/training are required, and what are the company's needs.
- **The industry in which you will be working.** How big is the industry? What are the biggest companies in the industry? What are the challenges facing the industry as a whole? Is the industry growing? Knowing this information, even though it may not be asked during the interview, will help you feel comfortable and confident.
- **The company with which you will be interviewing.** What is the company's history? What does the company do or sell? What sets it apart from the competition? What are the strengths and weaknesses of the company? Who would be your boss? What challenges is the company facing in the future?
- **The person who will be interviewing you.** Find out the title of the person interviewing you, as well as his or her responsibilities within the company. Start thinking about what questions you will ask this person.

> ## ⤷ TIPS
>
> Research resources:
>
> - Visit the employer's website, in addition to the websites of the employer's main competition.
> - Read company-issued press releases, company newsletters, and industry-specific magazines or websites.
> - Use social media—LinkedIn, Facebook, Twitter—to search for companies and people you may know.
> - Check the Chamber of Commerce in your city or town.
> - Speak directly with people who already work for the company or in that industry.
> - For a civil service position: obtain information from the agency's websites or contact the department directly.

## Rehearsing Your Material

Even if you can't perfectly predict what an interviewer will ask you, it's a safe bet he or she will want to know about your previous job experience, how the responsibilities you've had in the past will translate to the position for which you're interviewing, a time you excelled at work, a time you overcame a challenge or conflict, and what you can bring to the table at this particular organization. The research you've done on this job and this company will help with some of the answers, but it's up to you to make the most out of your personal history.

Practice with a friend or family member—ask them to ask you an open-ended question and see how well you can tell an anecdote that demonstrates an ability you have or a skill you acquired. Try to identify at least one specific story from each job that you can use to illustrate why you're a great fit for this company. Use your resume as a starting point to jog your memory if you need to. Your interviewer will want to hear you think on your feet in order to assess your communication skills, and you can show off both your memory and your self-awareness by having relevant anecdotes already drafted and rehearsed.

# Choose the Right Thing to Wear

Your appearance greatly affects an employer's first impression of you. Never wait until the last minute to choose your interview outfit, accessories, or hairstyle. What should you wear to an interview? A lot depends on the company's established dress code and culture. Your main goal is to look professional. No matter who you are, where you live, what job you are applying for, or what type of company you are visiting, your outfit should be clean, well tailored, flattering, and wrinkle free.

### What to Wear—Men
- a well-tailored, clean, and pressed suit in conservative, dark shades of navy blue, gray, or brown
- in a non-corporate environment, an acceptable alternative for a suit is a (less formal) sport jacket/blazer and dress slacks
- a pressed white or light-colored, long-sleeved, cotton dress shirt
- a tie that coordinates with your suit, avoiding wild colors and patterns
- dark socks that coordinate with your suit and dress shoes
- polished, plain black or brown leather dress shoes

### What to Wear—Women
Women can be a bit more creative in their wardrobe selection, as long as it fits within the company's dress code. You can look equally professional in a tailored dress or a blouse with a skirt or dress

slacks. Hosiery, depending on the season and region, is an important consideration. In addition:

- polished, plain, sensible pumps, or low-heeled dress shoes
- natural-looking makeup
- simple and understated jewelry that complements your outfit without attracting attention

### What to Avoid—Men
- jewelry, other than a watch and wedding band
- baseball caps or other hats

### What to Avoid—Women
- low-cut necklines, sleeveless tops, and sheer fabrics
- mini-skirts
- loud prints and patterns
- open-toed shoes and spike heels
- dramatic makeup and distracting nail polish
- excessive or flashy jewelry; overtly religious symbols

### General
- Make sure that you wash and neatly style your hair
- Be sure to wear deodorant/antiperspirant
- Clean and trim your nails
- Avoid fragrance of any kind—scents can cause allergic reactions in others or may be considered unappealing by your interviewer
- Body piercings: Wear small, simple earrings; no dangling earrings
- Tattoos: Your pre-interview research will tell you whether the office culture is likely to be accepting of tattoos; consider covering them if the workplace seems to be conservative.

# What to Bring

When you are stressed about your interview, it's easy to forget to bring something with you. Here is a list of everything you'll likely need:

- Several extra copies of your resume, letters of recommendation, and your list of references
- Your daily planner, phone, or tablet (so you can easily schedule additional appointments)
- Folder containing company research materials, a notebook, and two working pens
- Any additional materials (such as writing samples, portfolios, clips) requested by the interviewer or included in your application

All of these items will fit into a briefcase or portfolio. Write down the company's name, interviewer's name, address, telephone number, and directions to the location of the interview the night before. This way, there's no chance of losing or misplacing vital information.

# Common Types of Interviews

Potential employers can use many interview styles to get to know you better. Some interviews are done in a private office, on a one-to-one basis. Some interviews are done over the telephone or Skype, or over lunch or dinner at a restaurant. Following are descriptions of the most common types of interviews.

### One-on-One Interview

This is the most common type of interview. It involves two people—you and the interviewer. Most likely, you will be sitting opposite each other in an office or conference room while participating in a two-way conversation. However, these interviews can sometimes happen off-site (such as over a meal in a restaurant) or even over the telephone or Skype.

### Human Resources Screening Interview

Often, a representative from an employer's human resources department will interview you before you meet with the hiring manager. The screening interview ensures that you are right for the job. Inappropriate candidates (people who are obviously unprepared, unprofessional, etc.) are "screened out." This first step saves the hiring manager's time.

### Group Interview

While this may seem unusual, it is actually a common format, especially for big companies doing campus recruiting. If you are asked to participate in a group interview alongside several other applicants, your main priority is to make the most out of the attention you get. When it is your turn to respond to a question, it is your opportunity to make yourself stand out from the other applicants. Describe your marketable attributes clearly and concisely, and display your enthusiasm for the job and the company. In this situation, you will have less time to win over the interviewer, but at the same time, you can size up the "competition." Never be rude or interrupt fellow applicants.

### Panel Interview

During a panel interview, you will meet with several people at the same time. This type of interview simulates a business meeting at which you are the presenter. Members of the panel may be individuals with whom you would interact on the job or individuals designated by the company as a hiring committee or employee search group. The panel may include your potential supervisor and/or a human resources representative.

Being interviewed by a panel of people adds a bit more of a challenge to your interview. You now need to impress two, three, or more people at once. In addition to intelligently answering the questions posed to you and asking insightful questions, it is vital that you maintain eye contact and develop a rapport with each interviewer. Do not allow yourself to become intimidated in this situation. The interviewers know a panel interview format adds pressure, and they want to see how you will react. Try to give the panelists equal time. Providing thorough answers to each question ensures that you've given respectful, thoughtful answers to each member. Remember to be flexible and to demonstrate that you can think on your feet. If you go into the interview having done your research and are totally prepared, it will not matter if one person or five people are conducting the interview.

## The Second Interview

Sometimes, the interview process is a long one and can be spread out over more than one day. If you are invited back for a second interview, expect the interviewer to ask you more detailed and specific questions that directly relate to the job you are applying to fill. If you are invited for a second or third interview, you will know the employer is interested in you. Your job now is to say everything in your power to convince him or her to hire you.

Do not be surprised if you are introduced to other executives within the company during and after the second (and third) interviews. Also, the formats of subsequent interviews might change. The second interview, for example, might be held over lunch at a restaurant or be conducted as a panel interview.

Whatever style or format your second and third interviews are, you must be prepared. Do not get lazy and think of the additional interviews as just a formality. As the interview process goes on, the importance of each interview actually increases, so do your best every time.

# Top 25 Interview Mistakes

1. **Showing up late.** Be sure to allow yourself ample time to get to your interview. You must factor in unexpected circumstances, such as train delays or heavy traffic. If you know you're going to be late, call to let your interviewer know.

2. **Being unprepared to describe your experiences.** An interview is a test—and you should never walk into a test unprepared. Take some time to prepare your rehearsed responses, and think about how you will handle the questions your interviewer might ask. Practice describing your experiences aloud or conduct practice interviews with a partner.

3. **Answering questions with only a *yes* or *no*.** Your interviewer needs to get to know you, and he or she will be unable to do that if you don't volunteer information about yourself. Be sure to support your answers with examples.

4. **Fidgeting.** If you are tapping your foot, playing with a bracelet on your wrist, or constantly shifting in your seat, you won't look professional. And if you don't look professional, you won't get hired.

5. **Speaking too quickly.** You may want to get in a lot of information, but you don't want to speak so fast that your interviewer can't understand you. Take a deep breath before you begin answering questions and slow yourself down. Conduct practice interviews with a friend to make sure that your speaking voice is steady and even.

6. **Avoiding eye contact.** If you avoid making eye contact, you will be unable to establish a personal connection with your interviewer. You should be attentive and engaged in what your interviewer is saying.

7. **Not researching the company.** Q: "What do you know about our firm?" A: "Uh . . . not much." Answers like this will not get you hired.

8. **Lying.** Don't lie about or embellish your job experiences or academic record. Your interviewer is going to check these things out. If an interviewer catches you lying, you won't be hired. If your employer finds out about your misrepresentation after you've been hired, you will be fired—it's as simple as that.

9. **Not answering the question asked.** You want to highlight your experiences in the interview, but you should be careful to always answer the question being asked. Don't be so intent on launching into a great story about you that you avoid the question altogether—your interviewer will notice.

10. **Revealing too much.** Your interviewer is neither your best friend nor your therapist. She wants to learn about the skills and qualities you will bring to a job. She does not want to hear about your personal life or problems.

11. **Not "selling" yourself when you answer questions.** You should answer questions in a way that brings out the qualities that will serve you on the job. If you are asked how your best friend would describe you, say something like, "I think my best friend would describe me as loyal and dependable. People always know that they can count on me."

12. **Speaking poorly of, or belittling, past job experiences.** Disparaging other employers or jobs will make you sound unprofessional, negative, and hostile. And it will make the interviewer wonder what you would say about his or her company to others. Try to focus on what you learned from other jobs.

13. **Dressing too casually.** Your interviewer wants to hire a responsible professional. Make sure you look like one.

14. **Not asking any questions about the company.** By asking some good questions, you will prove that you are very interested in the job—and that you were motivated enough to research the position and the company.

15. **Not thanking the interviewer at the end of the interview.** In the business world, a little courtesy goes a long way. Your interviewer will appreciate and notice your good manners.

16. **Forgetting to send a thank you note.** Demonstrate your professionalism and courtesy by sending a note. You will also be more likely to stand out in your interviewer's mind if he or she has a reminder of the interview.

17. **Forgetting to bring extra resumes to the interview.** You may be asked for another copy of your resume, and you may have to submit an extra copy with any forms you have to fill out. Make sure that you are prepared.

18. **Neglecting to prepare a list of references.** Type up your references (with contact information) for your interviewer. He or she will not be interested in taking down all the names and numbers by hand, and it will be an inconvenience if you have to send the information at a later date.

19. **Forgetting the interviewer's name.** You should always bring a note pad (preferably in a professional leather portfolio) to an interview. Write down the interviewer's name if you think you won't be able to remember it. Thank the interviewer by name at the end of the interview.

20. **Going to an interview on an empty stomach.** You will feel more alert if you've had a nutritious meal, and you won't get hungry if the interview ends up lasting longer than you had anticipated. And, of course, you won't have to worry about your stomach rumbling in the middle of a question.

21. **Using slang.** Nothing makes you sound more unprofessional than peppering your speech with *like* and *y'know*. If you can't speak like a professional, your interviewer will question whether he or she can trust you to interact with clients or supervisors.

22. **Chewing gum, eating, or smoking.** These are obvious no-nos.

23. **Answering your cell phone.** Turn off your cell phone before you get to the interview.

24. **Interrupting the interviewer or talking excessively.** Don't ramble or go off on tangents. You want to showcase yourself and give the interviewer a good sense of your accomplishments, but make sure you don't cut the interviewer off or preclude him or her from asking questions. He or she has limited time to speak with you.

25. **Freezing up.** Relax! It's only an interview. If you are well prepared, you should feel confident and stress free. Smile and be yourself.

## Just Before the Interview

When you get to the interview (15 minutes early), do these final things:

- Visit the restroom (if for no other reason than to check your hair, tie knot, or lipstick in the mirror)
- Glance at your notes to refresh your memory
- Scan a corporate publication, newspaper, or trade magazine if offered in the reception area
- Smile and be polite to everyone you encounter
- Practice deep, calming breaths
- Visualize yourself having a great interview

# During the Interview

Though every interview you participate in will be unique, most interviews have five stages:

1. Introductions
2. Small talk
3. Exchanging information
4. Summarizing
5. Closing

Practice each stage at home, recording yourself on video or enlisting the help of a friend who can give you feedback on each stage. Be sensitive to your interviewers' transitions from one section to another; if it seems like they're beginning to wrap up, don't try to prolong the interview unnecessarily.

Take some time to review these guidelines, which are essential for succeeding on any interview.

- Get a good night's sleep before the interview so that you are awake and alert. You want to look and feel rested.
- The morning of your interview, read the local news and/or watch a morning news program. Be aware of the day's news events and be able to discuss them with the interviewer. Many interviewers like to start an interview with general chit chat. You want to appear knowledgeable about what is happening in the world around you.
- Before you enter the building for an interview, turn off your cell phone. In addition, turn off any alarms you have set. It is unacceptable to interrupt any interview with annoying sounds.
- Arrive at the interview alone. This may seem obvious, but even if a parent, significant other, or friend drove you to the interview or commuted with you for moral support,

leave him or her outside. You want to appear confident, not codependent.

- Arrive early for your interview, no matter what. Ideally, you want to arrive about 10–15 minutes early and check in with the receptionist. Don't arrive too early, though. Interviewers often have back-to-back meetings or other priorities. Arriving too early can be misinterpreted as not respecting the interviewer's carefully arranged schedule for the day.

- Keep in mind that you are being evaluated on every move you make. Often, even the receptionists or assistants have input on the hiring process, so always act professionally. Be polite, courteous, and friendly to everyone you encounter.

- When you are introduced to the interviewer, stand up, smile, make direct eye contact, and shake hands. Refer to the interviewer formally, as *Mr./Ms./Dr.* (insert last name).

- Throughout the interview, always try to maintain as much eye contact as possible and avoid fidgeting. The interviewer is probably trained to read your body language.

- You may be offered a drink at the start of the interview. Accept whatever is offered. To avoid caffeine, consider asking for water. If you are at a lunch or dinner meeting and the employer offers you an alcoholic beverage, decline, but ask for something nonalcoholic.

- Even if the interviewer takes a casual approach to the interview, you are still being evaluated, so never lose focus. Pay attention to the conversation, keep smiling, maintain eye contact, answer all questions openly and honestly, and use complete sentences. Never answer questions with a one-word answer of yes or no.

- Always think before you speak. Your interviewer asks every question—even if it seems to have no relevance to anything—for a reason. Some employers like to see how you will react to bizarre questions and to see if you can think on your feet.

- If you do not know the answer to a specific question, never lie or make up an answer. Never say, "I don't know." When you feel stuck, pause. Take a breath. Say, "Let me think about that for a moment," and proceed when you feel calm and prepared. What may seem like an eternity to you will come across as a contemplative, thought-gathering moment to the interviewer.
- At your initial interview, you should not ask about salary, benefits, or vacation time. You can bring up these topics once the interviewer offers you the job or expresses a very strong interest in hiring you—not before.
- During the later part of your interviews, be sure to affirm that you are interested in the job for which you are applying. Explain exactly why you want the job, what you can offer to the company, and why you are the best candidate to fill the position.

# After the Interview

## Send a Thank You Note

Sending a short, personalized thank you note within 24 hours after an interview is an absolute must. Send it to the interviewer via email or as a legibly handwritten or typed note. In your note, make a specific reference to something you discussed during the interview (to refresh the interviewer's mind about who you are) and explain in a sentence or two how excited you are about the possibility of working for the company.

- **The typed letter.** Using the same letterhead and paper that you created for your resume, type out a brief, professional letter on a computer. Print it out, and send it in a matching envelope. Don't forget the stamp!

- **The handwritten note.** Some people prefer a personal touch. Don't make the mistake of using casual language in the note: be specific, be direct, and be professional. Also, it is a good idea to gather your thoughts and edit on scrap paper, then copy the finished note onto quality stationery. Many interviewers appreciate a handwritten note; however, if you are interviewing in a conservative industry, use a typed letter instead.

### Sample Interview Follow-Up and Thank You Note

Linda uses her letter to outline how her accomplishments meet or exceed the ideal candidate qualifications discussed during her interview.

**Linda Jameson**
2123 Lincoln Avenue, Apt 3D, Minneapolis, MN 55555
555-555-1234
linda.jameson@yourdomain.com

May 14, 2015

William Sanders
Prudential Financial Services
600 U.S. 169
St. Louis Park, MN 55555

Dear Mr. Sanders:

Thank you very much for the time and opportunity to meet with you this past Thursday. Our discussion was enlightening and deepened my interest in the Prudential Financial team. I remain confident that my qualifications are a strong match for your needs, and I hope to be among those in consideration for the position of Financial Services Associate.

My Bachelor of Arts degree in Finance from Northeastern University, combined with my three years of experience at MetLife, has provided me with the right background to become an asset to Prudential. During my time at MetLife, I have collaborated with my team members to achieve company goals and maintain relationships with a broad client base. I continue to expand my capabilities by enrolling in relevant educational programs in my personal time. Joining the Prudential team would allow me to grow and be challenged in a successful environment.

Thank you, once again, for your time. I will remain available for further interviews as needed. I look forward to hearing from you again soon.

Sincerely,

Linda Jameson

### *Follow Up*

After the interview and depending on the next steps discussed at the close of the interview, you should follow up. Generally, the recommendation is to follow up three to five business days after the interview, either by telephone or email.

## ⇨ TIPS

To set yourself apart from other candidates, send a thank you note via email immediately following the interview and also send a note on your stationery or bonded resume-quality paper via standard mail.

# APPENDIX II: WORKPLACE DOS AND DON'TS

You've gotten the job offer, filled out all the paperwork, and read through the company orientation manual. Now what?

## Your First Day in the Office

Your supervisor or a new colleague will most likely show you around. Depending on the size of the company, this may be as simple as pointing out the communal kitchen, the bathroom, and the network printers, or as elaborate as a tour of multiple floors of an office building to learn where various departments are. Although either tour will probably include a visit to the office supply cabinet, make sure you bring something to write with and something to write on. If you're invited to attend meetings right away, sit back and observe; it's usually better to ask questions from your immediate supervisor or office neighbor to catch up later instead of disrupting an ongoing discussion. Draw yourself a seating chart to record your new coworkers names and where they sat—it will help you to put names with faces. Jotting down some notes of what was said will also help to get you up to speed.

Joining a new company often means learning what systems are already in place. Whom do you report to? How are you given new assignments? Do you get to determine what you work on and when, or will your supervisor be managing your day-to-day tasks? You can't meet or exceed expectations if you don't know what they are first!

## Dos

- **Ask questions!**
- **Take initiative:** This doesn't mean going rogue or being resistant to existing company practices, but you can demonstrate that you're an independent thinker by coming up with your own way to complete an assignment and running it by your supervisor to get his or her approval. If your supervisor wants to redirect you, be receptive to the feedback, but perhaps he or she will appreciate that you're already thinking of ways to innovate.
- **Get to know your neighbors:** Don't be distracting or monopolize their time, but set a goal of introducing yourself to one coworker a day until you know everyone on your team or anyone with whom your department interacts regularly. Even just a few moments of chatting as you finish a first cup of coffee can help you develop working relationships with your colleagues.
- **Volunteer for projects:** Obviously this should be cleared with your supervisor, but a great way to expand your responsibilities in a new position is to be willing to take on new challenges. If one of your superiors is looking for

someone to lead a new project or supervise the execution of a new initiative, consider whether your workload could accommodate an addition. It's almost always better to be the person who says "Yes, I can handle that for you—anything else?" rather than the person who sits silently while an opportunity passes him or her by.

# Don'ts

- **Complain:** Even if your old office gave out free coffee and omelets every morning and your new office only offers stale animal crackers, you should approach your first weeks on the job with a continuation of your best interview behavior. Don't let your reputation become that of somebody who finds fault with everything, who gripes instead of saying good morning, or who is convinced the grass was greener on the other side of the fence.
- **Act helpless:** If you're really and truly stuck with something, you can always ask for help instead of wasting time struggling under the radar. But with run-of-the-mill technology issues, small-scale office-related needs, or new software to learn, try to cultivate a sense of self-sufficiency where you can. Needy employees can become a distraction to coworkers or signal to the boss that they're not ready for more responsibility.
- **Get too comfortable too quickly:** Many workplaces allow employees to customize their workspaces in some ways; others prefer to keep shared spaces uncluttered and uniform. Be aware of the prevailing office culture and do your best not to disrupt it by being too loud, letting your personal effects creep onto someone else's desk, or bringing in too many photos or knick knacks from home. Establish yourself as a professional first and an animal or sports enthusiast second.

- **Violate or mock HR policies:** Whether your orientation was a quick spin around the office complex or a more formal company-wide presentation, the guidelines presented by your HR rep were given to you for a reason. You can demonstrate your professionalism by taking them seriously, from the basics—like adhering to a dress code—to the legal standards of conduct—like refraining from making personal comments about your coworkers.

# ADDITIONAL ONLINE PRACTICE

Using the codes below, you'll be able to log in and access additional online practice materials!

**Your free online practice access codes are:**

LELCOLT090

LELALCT064

LELCOLT092

LELT186

LELT188

Follow these simple steps to redeem your codes:

- Go to **www.learningexpresshub.com/affiliate** and have your access codes handy.

**If you're a new user:**

- Click the **New user? Register here** button and complete the registration form to create your account and access your products.
- Be sure to enter your unique access codes only once. If you have multiple access codes, you can enter them all—just use a comma to separate each codes.
- The next time you visit, simply click the **Returning user? Sign in** button and enter your username and password.
- Do not re-enter previously redeemed access codes. Any products you previously accessed are saved in the **My Account** section on the site. Entering a previously redeemed access codes will result in an error message.

**If you're a returning user:**

- Click the **Returning user? Sign in** button, enter your username and password, and click **Sign In**.
- You will automatically be brought to the **My Account** page to access your products.
- Do not re-enter previously redeemed access codes. Any products you previously accessed are saved in the **My Account** section on the site. Entering a previously redeemed access codes will result in an error message.

**If you're a returning user with a new access codes:**

- Click the **Returning user? Sign in** button, enter your username, password, and new access codes, and click **Sign In**.
- If you have multiple access codes, you can enter them all—just use a comma to separate each codes.
- Do not re-enter previously redeemed access codes. Any products you previously accessed are saved in the **My Account** section on the site. Entering a previously redeemed access codes will result in an error message.

If you have any questions, please contact LearningExpress Customer Support at LXHub@LearningExpressHub.com. All inquiries will be responded to within a 24-hour period during our normal business hours: 9:00 A.M.–5:00 P.M. Eastern Time. Thank you!

# NOTES